Reflections on Espionage

Reflections On Espionage

The Question of *Cupcake*

by John Hollander

Yale University Press New Haven and London

A somewhat shorter version of this book appeared in *Poetry*, November 1974, volume CXXV, Number 2. Other portions were first published in *The Carolina Quarterly* and *The Ohio Review*.

Printed in the United States of America.

Library of Congress Cataloging-in-Publication Data
Hollander, John.
Reflections on espionage : the question of Cupcake / John Hollander.
p. cm.
ISBN 0-300-07966-4 (alk. paper)
1. Espionage poetry.   I. Title.
PS3515.03485R4   1999
811'.54—dc21   99-44253

A catalogue record for this book is available from the British Library.
The paper in this book meets the guidelines for permanence and durability of the Committee on Production Guidelines for Book Longevity of the Council on Library Resources.

10 9 8 7 6 5 4 3 2 1

To the memory of Lionel Trilling

Introduction

When *Reflections on Espionage* first appeared, one reviewer—
Louis Martz, who had himself been in O.S.S.—remarked
that it was derived from "the recent [this was 25 years ago]
flurry of revelations and counter-revelations about the Sec-
ond World War as represented in John Masterman's *The
Double-Cross System*." To some degree it was certainly true.
But this book had, like many others, a number of origins,
in both my dispositions and my reading. From college years
on, I had wanted to keep a journal but had abandoned each
attempt after a few consecutive days. Though writing a
twentieth-century equivalent of a sonnet sequence seemed
uncertain, I longed for a poetic task that could define itself
in that sort of continuous commitment. During the early
nineteen seventies, I had been reading David Kahn's monu-
mental history of cryptanalysis, *The Code Breakers,* as well as
The Double-Cross System in the American edition introduced
by Norman Holmes Pearson, who had been a senior col-
league at Yale (I was living and teaching in New York at
the time). It was the story of how many German spies sent
into England in World War II had been turned into doubles.
Though the subject was fascinating, what continued to
haunt me was peripheral to the central matter. It was the
cryptonyms, or cover names, of the agents under consider-
ation—"Garbo," "Balloon," "Tricycle" (the cover name
of the celebrated double agent Dusak Popov)—that de-
lighted me for their free play of cryptic onomastic signifiers.
Long before writing anything about it, I'd imagined a sort
of *espion manqué*, a somewhat bumbling, somewhat distracted
spy whose cryptonym would be "Cupcake" (a slightly
tougher, denser version of the morally metaphorical term
"Creampuff").
   In 1972 I wrote a short poem called "Cupcake to Lyre-
bird" ("Lyrebird" being a mythological rather than an or-

nithological construction—a sort of Orphean figure, a muse-like presence—and Cupcake's case agent, purely ad hoc to this poem). In it, Cupcake is *not* doing his work, but rather staring at an uncompleted jigsaw puzzle, possibly suggested by a wonderful long poem of James Merrill's called "Lost in Translation" that he had recently read to me. Merrill's poem involved a jigsaw puzzle remembered from child-hood and its Proustian extensions into matters of life and art and language. My poem (which eventually became the 9/17 entry in *Reflections*) invoked a puzzle remembered from my own childhood. It formed itself in purely syllabic lines of eleven syllables, for no particular emblematic reason (I was writing mostly syllabic verse at the time). After being written, it was put away.

Some months later, I presented "Cupcake to Lyrebird," with a brief introductory account, at a reading in Washington, D.C., and was delightedly surprised when a poet and scholar named Edward Weismiller approached me after the reading to say that certain things in the poem rang true for him as a former O.S.S. man. At the time, we talked of Norman Pearson, and it was then that I learned that Pearson's O.S.S. cryptonym had been "Puritan." (In 1968, Weismiller had published a wonderful spy novel, as much a study of innocence as a narrative of espionage, called *Serpent Sleeping*.)

Following that reading, the poem languished, appeared in a little magazine, and came to life again a year later, at a sad time for me, in the autumn of 1973. I'd been unable to write much all that fall. One of the sources of my malaise was the death of W. H. Auden. My family and I had visited him in Austria six weeks before. His dying and the Yom Kippur war in Israel had almost coincided. Auden had meant a great deal to me—I had read his work since my freshman year at college, and I have always felt that he, preceded by George Bernard Shaw and followed by George Orwell, had been one of my moral mentors at a distance (he was the only one of the three I knew at all—we had met when

I was still an undergraduate, and we got to know one another in the early sixties). Whenever I have been free of political callowness, it is partly as a result of reading their work.

Some months after that autumn 1973, the phrase "daily twilight messages" in "Cupcake to Lyrebird" caught my eye; the notion of *having* to send something (i.e., write something) every day spoke to my malaise. I brooded on the poem, then resurrected Cupcake and started him out again, thinking that if I could have him send off regular transmissions, on pain of death or disclosure, something might come of it. (The concretely imagined scene had, I suppose, been suggested by images of secret agents such as those in the film version of Graham Greene's *Ministry of Fear,* who climbed up to an attic room, selected the appropriate crystals, and transmitted encrypted text by means of 1943 state-of-the-art equipment.)

I started with a kind of narrative doodle—"Cupcake here. Hardly anything to report / Today . . ."—having indeed no idea what I'd be writing about. But I immediately populated the "transmission" with the quickly improvised names of other agents—"Thumbtack," "Maisie," etc. Into this group I idly dropped an "actual" notional name, "Allen Aspirin" (see the note to transmission 1/14). The next day, there seemed no need to doodle. Cupcake's second "transmission," on 1/15, was the first to have any real "substance," both in what was starting to unfold as a fictional world, and with regard to my own life, rather than Cupcake's. The first matter "to report" was the death of a great agent—partly, I suppose, to confirm for myself a spy = writer allegory that seemed to be developing. "Steampump" was Auden, who had died the previous September. I called him "Steampump" because by his own reiterated admission, a toy pumping-engine he'd had in childhood was his first object of desire: "When I was young I /Loved a pumping-engine, / Thought it every bit as/ Beautiful as you" ("Heavy Date"). It was the personal matter of what his life had meant for me particularly over the previous fifteen years or so, coming together with the poet-as-agent in this vignette, that made me realize what the central fiction of this sequence would be. The next thirty transmissions were written almost daily. My own equivalent of "sending" them was to mail a carbon copy of each, with no comment, to my friend and critic Harold Bloom. He was puzzled for a few days, but then seemed to get the point.

I observed earlier that I have never been able to keep a journal, but in this case Cupcake's transmissions allowed John Hollander to record occasional details from his own life intertwined with purely fictional ones from Cupcake's. I could speak, through some encoded distancing, of my own writing in progress. Bits of daily trivia crept into Cupcake's world, and they and the fictions began to give substance to one another. When cross with or disappointed in something a friend had done, I could mention this with a coded name; my views of living poets could emerge in terms of the pastoral-like coding of spies = writers (as opposed to shepherd swains = writers, but more of this shortly). But this was a very minor matter: the fiction itself was the major one, always. Although deeply attached to Conrad's *Secret Agent* and to narratives of Graham Greene, Eric Ambler, and particularly John Le Carré, I had no intention of parodying the fiction of espionage novels. I was merely systematically bungling it, as far as suspense and credible detail were concerned, but bungling it as poetry always bungles the expository or narrative forms it may explore. Cupcake spends too much time brooding about meta-espionage, deriving parables from the facts of tradecraft, and nearly allegorizing himself out of existence.

During the course of composing the transmissions that constitute the poem, I decided that Cupcake was an art historian and museum curator, and all sorts of personal details—such as the blue faïence hippopotamus at the Metropolitan Museum of Art (see transmission 1/23), a reproduction of which I'd given my children—got worked in. I should add that I knew nothing at the time of Anthony

Blunt's spying for the Soviet Union—I found those revelations years later to be eerily parallel to the writings of Cupcake. For it then seemed that the poem represented a case not so much of life imitating art as of art unwittingly imitating life—that Cupcake's career seemed to have invented, in its forms alone, Blunt's. Cupcake's cover life also represented the doubling of art and life. As the poem developed, this doubling was again reflected in the relation, in the book as it developed, of poetic *technê* and tradecraft, and, ultimately, by poetry as an allegory for all productive human work, as reflected in the different senses of "work" (particularly, *opus, oeuvre,* and, more generally, the continuing activity of the human condition). This allegory probably haunts all my poetry.

The decision to compose a unified poem was a drawn-out one; the shape of the whole thing dawned on me only in the first month. Early on, it emerged as a form of pastoral, and thus introduced the two pastoral eclogues: the 1/27 transmission, a version of Theocritus's second idyll, in which a girl casts a spell with a prayer wheel to bring her lover back (here, tape machine spools are used instead); and the more Virgilian transmission of 1/28. I slowly realized that transmissions could be lyrical, meditative, or satiric. The deeper matters of what espionage might mean—for any individual imaginative consciousness nonetheless leading an ordinarily institutional life—kept emerging during the course of the writing. But there is another aspect of pastoral fiction here. For historical scholars like Christopher Hill, Milton's neo-pastoral coding was all political (it was to keep his anti-royalist and radically protestant sympathies and sympathetic friends hidden from the cops). A kind of kindergarten-level ends and means debate takes place in the eclogue of transmission 1/28, yet the "we/they" is an aesthetic and moral trope. Although my concerns were never political, I was amused as well as delighted (for Cupcake's allegorical deep cover, as well as for other obvious reasons) that *The Washington Monthly* gave *Reflections on Espionage* one of its three annual Political Book Awards (in

March 1977, along with books by John Morton Blum and John Dean). But if anything, the poem's quasi-pastoral mode substituted another realm for the political one (rather than even allegorizing politics). Nevertheless, a notion of the political brought me up short, as I realized that the title I'd given the poem had echoed that of Georges Sorel's *Réflexions sur la violence*. Perhaps the rhetorical paradigm and the minimizing of ideology by that syndicalist author (unread since college) lay beneath my title. Among the many uses of "politics"—particularly in phrases like "the politics of [X or Y]" by academics writing ostensibly about literature today—perhaps some might be applied here. But I had, and have, none of these in mind.

Almost from the start (by the sixth transmission), it seemed that Cupcake's distracting concerns with cryptography and its possible significances should be kept from Lyrebird (who was at that point no longer simply a case agent, but perhaps a head of poetic station). I decided to have Cupcake send unauthorized transmissions to another agent, "Image." All the messages actually mailed to Harold Bloom (for purported transmission to "Lyrebird") didn't touch on ciphers, even as my years of discussions of poetry with him hadn't engaged matters of form (perhaps a crucial part of poetic tradecraft). Cupcake's debilitating need to chatter on about cryptography paralleled mine to understand poetic form, with meter metonymically representing all such issues. His first transmission to Image (on 1/19) discussed an "eleven by eleven grid"—the eleven-syllabled line in which the original "Cupcake to Lyrebird" poem was written, and which was subsequently kept to throughout, 1/19 being uniquely eleven lines long. The "Image" transmissions were actually all sent to James Merrill ("Image" = "Jimmy"), whose responses in return are reprinted in the note to 9/28. The complex senses of "code" in English—cipher, *nomos,* regimen, and so forth—were important. Encipherment generally also suggested such older poetic notions as emblematics and the doctrine of signatures, and such acutely present ones as that of the plain text of experience enciphered in trope itself figuring the central poetic matter of trope being enciphered (post-structuralist babble had not yet come up with its ubiquitous term "inscribed") in pattern of scheme; of Frostian ulteriority; of another aspect of the overall matter of private and public selves.

Another, personal, dimension was added by my recent interest in the history of cryptanalysis, and how it had caused me to recall my first childhood experience of it. Even before being old enough to have read of the similar breaking of simple substitution ciphers in Poe's "The Gold Bug" and the Sherlock Holmes story "The Adventure of the Dancing Men," I had listened to the quarter-hour afternoon children's radio program called "Little Orphan Annie" and had sent away, with "that thin, round, aluminum seal from underneath the lid of a can of [the sponsoring] Ovaltine," for a "decoder pin," a small badge with a rotating disk and a number of different simply keyed number-for-letter ciphers. At the end of particular episodes, some clue about what would happen in the next was broadcast. The first one I remember deciphering was CAPTAIN AND MEN ABANDON SHIP (I had to ask my father what "abandon" meant).

Of course, Cupcake's messages to another agent ("Image") about whom Lyrebird was never told (but who, of course, discovered this by other undisclosed means) constituted a betrayal and a compromise of what for his handlers was his status. Former spymaster (and, more recently, novelist of espionage) William Hood observed in his factual narrative *Mole* that "No espionage service can tolerate the merest whiff of independence or reserve on the part of an agent. For the spy, espionage is a one-way street." I understood this implicitly at the time, and after the first "Image" transmission I began to envision an ending to the whole sequence. Cupcake's correspondence with "Image"—and, later in the poem, to one "Grusha" (Richard Poirier)—seemed to assure his eventual demise. Cupcake's communication with two handlers gave me a small frisson: when first reading Kafka's *The Trial* in college, I found Joseph

K.'s contemplation of having two advocates disturbingly amusing, and I thought of what it would be like to have two psychoanalysts (I had only one), each kept secret from the other. There are a number of other agents whose actual counterparts could be identified, but the key was never really that important. Donald Davie sent me a detailed questionnaire in December 1974 about a possible elaborate allegory of literary-historical and stylistically polemical groups and factions. But that wasn't what the coding was for. A lot of it was playful, a way of making mere actuality metaphorical. Sometimes the cryptonyms designating actual persons (as opposed to "nulls," meaningless letters or numbers inserted in a ciphered text only to confuse) were generated by wordplay from their names (as with "Image" = Jimmy mentioned above). Thus: "Lac" (the inversion of "Cal," as Lowell was called by his friends) and "Lake" (from "Elinor Eastlake," or "Lakey," the character based on Bishop in Mary McCarthy's *The Group*) may have embodied my feelings at the time regarding some relation between the work of those two poets. The names "Moroz" and "Grusha" are Russian versions of their actual counterparts, but have no other significance. The poem was not to function as a literary roman à clef—that was only incidental.

Yet one episode transcribed from life may be worth mentioning. I have always had mixed feelings about Ezra Pound. In recalling Gertrude Stein's characterization of him as "a village explainer, great if you are a village, if not, not," it should be said that when young I was indeed a village, and Pound's poetry and its enigmas meant a great deal to me when I began to write. But I was never an idolizer and did not, as my friend Allen Ginsberg did at the time, write him fan letters when he was in St. Elizabeth's hospital. Richard Stern, who was living in Venice and visited Pound frequently at Olga Rudge's house in the Dorsoduro, invited me to accompany him there in winter 1963. Curiosity prodded me to accept. I found the old man in bed and subconversational, but I did transmit regards from Robert

Lowell and Norman Pearson to the precise effect narrated in transmission 5/9 (in which "Puritan" is Pearson and "Kilo" is Pound). When Pearson read the poem in its original form, he suggested that I send it to the celebrated James J. Angleton—then actively in charge of counterintelligence for the Central Intelligence Agency and in his earlier days a poet, devotee of Pound, and founder of the excellent literary quarterly *Furioso*. I ignored the suggestion at the time and did so only years later, after Pearson's death and Angleton's retirement. In return I received a kind note of acknowledgment from Angleton containing a photograph of the northern lake where he had been fishing and an inscription to the effect that this was all he did these days. Subsequently, on reading *Cloak and Gown,* Robin Winks's chronicle of the role that Yale and other universities have played in supplying personnel for intelligence work, I learned that Angleton's cryptonym had been "Fisherman." I don't know whether said Fisherman thought I knew this or would subsequently find it out.

When it became time to get rid of Cupcake and put an end to the transmissions, the metaphor of coding was led down into the literalness of encryption, which allowed an enciphered message—the only utterance from "Lyrebird"— to function as the agency of such a termination. That cipher text is simply "X" repeated, the key to which is a complex string of letters provided in transmissions 9/27 and 9/29. Cupcake's final overwrought transmission of 9/ 30 calls for his own destruction and entails a sort of superencipherment—the plain text is "coded" in a kind of encrypted acrostic (as explained in the note to it). This was clearly a way to end the poem's continuous trope of encoding by bringing it again back to the literal—to the world of the Little Orphan Annie Decoder Pin.

In revising and reordering some of the transmissions (labeled simply with dates roughly covering the months in which they were actually composed), I was able to incorporate the originating "Cupcake to Lyrebird," toward the end of the sequence, setting it up with transmissions 9/13 and 9/15. Daryl Hine, a brilliant poet and translator, was at that time the truly outstanding editor of the monthly magazine of verse *Poetry*, and he published the entire text as the November 1974 issue of that journal. The only notes were those to what are now transmissions 9/27 and 9/30. Two years later, when my beloved editor, the late Harry Ford, was about to bring it out as a book, twenty-eight transmissions were added, including two lengthy ones to "Grusha" and two that provided a narrative context for including the original "Cupcake to Lyrebird" poem. (For interested readers, the later additions were: 2/19 To Image; 2/27; 6/10 To Image; 6/15 To Bun; 6/26 To Grusha; 6/30 To Grusha; 7/3 To Grusha; 7/15 To Image; 7/15; 7/16; 7/18; 7/20; 7/21; 8/21; 8/22; 8/23; 8/25; 8/26; 8/27; 8/28; 8/29 To Image; 9/1 ; 9/8; 9/11; 9/12 To Image; 9/13; 9/15 To Lyrebird, Directly; 9/17 To Lyrebird.) The remaining notes were appended then; they have now been expanded for this new edition.

Returning to the question of sources and influences, it should be added that over the years I have come to see how much Auden's early (1932) quirky book *The Orators* may have haunted me, as well as his even earlier (1928) poem "The Secret Agent." Also, Cupcake's transmissions resonate with occasional tonal echoes of René Char's *Les Feuilles d'Hypnos*. Yet, a most problematic precursorship remains to be acknowledged—problematic because it is impossible for me to assess the importance to *Reflections* of a remarkable poem by Henri Coulette (1927-88) called "The War of the Secret Agents." Having first encountered it in 1964 (it was published in an anthology in which my work also appeared), I cannot remember now reading it through or how it affected me at the time. The poem is composed of a series of seventeen short dramatic monologues spoken by various members of a World War II network in Paris, as well as by their counter-espionage pursuer and a postwar historian. The sections frame a narrative, aided by an initial glossary dramatis personae which, like all the sections (including some footnotes) is in six-lined stanzas, each line purely syllabic in measure (11, 5, 7, 9, 10, 7, with an extra syllable sometimes allowed in lines 10 and 11). I do not remember noticing this on my original reading of the poem; indeed, my memory of the whole piece had shriveled into a recollection of ambiance, and a few names and incidents. But some things about the poem may have risen to the surface of my memory a decade later, for reading Coulette's poem last year made me feel that an unacknowledged debt had been incurred. For example, only on this second reading did it become clear that Coulette's monologue X is, unlike all the others, rhymed. More significantly, monologue XI, "Orphan Annie: The Broken Code" (no such cryptonym is mentioned elsewhere) consists of one stanza—six lines of strings of numbers between 1 and 20. Their simple-substitution cipher yields a broken-off warning that one person within the group is doubling for the Germans; as far as meter is concerned, when the digits are read aloud as cardinal numbers in English, the enunciation of each line comprises the correct number of syllables. My overlooked fraternity with Coulette in the matter of the Little Orphan Annie Decoder Pin charmed me on recent rereading. This sort of overlaid cipher system turns up a few times in connection with Cupcake's growing obsession with encipherment, and it now seems uncanny that I do not remember noticing much, or remembering much, on my first reading of "The War of the Secret Agents." I was always conscious of the presence of particular poems of Auden during the months of writing Cupcake's transmissions, but I am only now aware of how various elements of Coulette's poem conducted their covert operations within me. And I did not know until very recently that Coulette's secret agents ("Prosper," "Archambault," "Denise") were those of the "Prosper" network run by the British Special Operations Executive in France in 1943, compromised and wrapped up before the end of that year. Coulette had read about the network in Jean Overton Fuller's historical account, *Double Webs*.

With few exceptions, espionage has not been a matter

for poetry. When Ben Jonson was imprisoned under Elizabeth in 1598, two jailhouse informants were put next to him, but—as Drummond of Hawthornden observed—he was warned "by his keeper, and they got nothing from him." One of Jonson's epigrams (Epigram LIX: *On Spies*) refers to them:

> Spies, you are lights in state, but of base stuff,
> Who, when you've burnt yourselves down to the snuff,
> Stink, and are thrown away. End fair enough.

Jonson's contempt for this lowest form of intelligence-gathering life, and his exalted sense of the public role and responsibilities of the poet, would never allow him to associate the two. But only in modernity—with a century of romantic tradition behind it, however unacknowledged—could poetry then embrace questions of "silence, exile and cunning," enigmas and codes, depersonalization and impersonation, simulation and dissimulation (the paired pretenses of purporting to be some particular Other, and purporting not to be Oneself), overt and covert meanings and ways of life, to name only a few. Spies are actors in improvised scenarios, and case agents are their author-directors. *Actor* and *agent* have a common Latin ancestry, and secret agency—in the most general sense—invokes many aspects of poetic identity. The realm of modern institutionalized espionage is one in which legends are floated out into their world to deceive (not, as in the realm of poetry, transmitted for some kind of wonder); in which lies, at least of omission, are the fabric of life; in which pseudonyms denote notional entities in a complex but anti-poetic travesty of the logic of naming. In this world of espionage, Cupcake, his fellow agents, his controllers, and his world are all equally notional—nulls in some general cipher. For me, their invention was a poetic source only later to be realized as such.

I should add that an interview with Professor Wesley Wark in an issue of the Canadian magazine *Queen's Quar-*

terly devoted to matters of spying a few years ago led me to recall and formulate some of the circumstances and concerns governing the composition of *Reflections on Espionage*. I have drawn upon some of the material elicited by his astute questioning in this introduction.

Although I still have not been able to keep a diary, writing this poem has led me to create analogous sequential structures in subsequent poems. Certainly the narrative section of "Green" (from "Spectral Emanations"), "In Time," "On the Calendar," all of *Powers of Thirteen*, and "The Tesserae" descend from it in various ways. I remain grateful to Cupcake and am delighted to have him reappear, a bit less enigmatically, accompanied by some explanation.

About the master-spy whose code name was *Cupcake*, little is known that can be told. He worked for an altogether inconvenient little republic which ceased to exist a good time ago. The regular, encoded radio transmissions, copies of which were eventually recovered by sources in his native country, have only recently been deciphered, the eleven-phase transposition grid he used for enciphering his messages having been guessed at earlier but rejected as being too archaic. Cupcake must have employed other modes of communication with the many agents he mentions in these dispatches; but only those reports to his control, through the control to a director named Lyrebird, briefly to one Grusha, or, strangely enough, to the agent Image about whom nothing is known, have been preserved. All of these had been intercepted by Lyrebird. They are here reprinted in deciphered, but raw, form, unencumbered with more than a few glosses.

Reflections on Espionage

Cupcake here. Hardly anything to report
Today: the weather will be suitable
Only for what can be done in the morning
And on the outlying islands. I have paid
Thumbtack and Maisie and The Foot. Aspirin
May be going bad: yesterday he stared at
A coin for hours—I walked into the laundry
And found him staring at a coin—not ringing
It down on the stone tub, nor scratching at the
Milling around the edge, nor tilting the head
Side to see what the blue light bulb above him
Might do to the President's eyes. I took it
From him, but there was nothing in the date—it
Was not one of those—and when he finally
Gave me the shirt and I went home warily
It occurred to me that Aspirin perhaps
Should be discontinued sometime before March.
He broke his cover once when we were talking,
Referred to himself as *Allen Aspirin*,
And gave me something of a start. Tell Lyrebird
I must hear from him soon. That is all for now.

Steampump is gone. He died quietly in his
Hotel room and his sleep. His cover people
Attended to everything. What had to
Be burned was burned. He taught me, as you surely
Know, all that I know; yet I had to pass him
By in the Square at evening—in the soft
Light of wrought-iron lamps and the rich, cheerful
Shadows which rose up from the stones to meet it—
Without even our eyes having touched, without
Acknowledgment. And thereby, of course, we were
Working together. What kind of work is this
For which if we were to touch in the darkness

It would be without feeling the other there?
It might help to know whether Steampump's dying
Was part of the work or not. I shall not b e
Told, I know. Until next time, this is Cupcake.

1/16

No new movements of goods or men. Today was
Warmer and I walked downtown among office
Buildings that must be only partly rented—
Although I don't think this really important—
And found myself avoiding certain blocks and,
Particularly, certain corners. I may
Be needing a new cover. It is not just
Ridiculous accidents I fear: catching
A hand in the separator; prating
Of secrets in one's sleep; being arrested
In a case of mistaken identity;
Licking an envelope flap that a maddened
Writer of ever-rejected short fictions
Had poisoned; falling into a vat of hot
Milk chocolate—every job has its hazards;
These have all happened, as you know. I worry
Mostly, though, how having been made another
Person might have enabled me to do the
Work better, being another case: Do I
Suit the instance of myself we selected?
What would have been a better one? Signing off.

1/17

Reception has been weak and I have received
No questionnaire from you; I sat in my room
Past the appointed time, staring at dials
Whose readings I not only knew but as it
Were had written there, wondering what would be
Asked of me today. And while I waited

4

I fancied myself in a high collar and
Suit of a sixty-year-old cut gazing
At wireless equipment parts of which one
Buys today as *objets de virtù*, watching
My shiny coherer for activity
In the matter of such simple questions—
Naval signals, tonnages, the contents of
An archaic type of agreement or two.
Am I going to end up like Kidd, that old
Romancier who would have been happiest
Helping some Ottoman corner to totter?
(He did not report in this week, by the way)
Well, I suppose that our work is play enough.
Hoping that Lyrebird will get through, I remain .

1/18

A bit of transmission has been coming through,
But so disjointed that I cannot be sure
Whether I am to work more closely now with
Artifact, or terminate him (using the
Virus? It has worked very well). The weather
Is dry and very cold, and the reception
Should be better in this clear, cornflower-blue
Evening sky, low winds humming through icy
Wires above clusters of starlings cackling—
Not like the day's closing message outriding
A chattering posse of noise, but in that
System of the air in which the noise is part
Of the very signal. Come in, Lyrebird: for
I have started to brood about Artifact.

1/19 (TO IMAGE)

Cupcake to Image: They are not aware of
My contact with you; but there are reports, or
Rather resonances of the writing of

5

Reports for which I cannot use the usual
Frequencies, insinuations they'd not take to:
For instance, this eleven by eleven
Grid I am using seems to dictate to me
Messages it might most lovingly encode,
As an eternal form of water-jar might
Whisper to some monk in a cold, white room the
Secrets of size, color of glaze. More later.

1/19

I have not been in touch with anyone else
For some days, save for Artifact, of course (I
Still await further instructions there) and for
Felucca, whom I visited in the way
We had agreed upon. Her warm studio
Looks out over the cold bare park where skaters
Crowd the gray ice; we worked it out about the
Pictures and how to send them, she gave me some
Milk and whiskey punch and I stayed on through most
Of the evening (yes, from time to time I
Fuck Felucca, but I suppose you know that).
There is a strange aura above wide streets at
Nightfall: the quality of human movement
Seems somehow different from what I later
Remember of it—in any event, I
Felt this strange pace in this strange alteration
Of light on my way back this evening, and
So report it for what it may be worth.

1/20 (TO IMAGE)

To Image (more on the nature of the grid):
One comes, I suppose, to love the ciphers as
One loves the messages lurking inside them—
"Come at five. He will be away till Friday";
"Satisfactory, Cupcake. Their whole Southern

6

Operation has come unstuck"; "Good news. It's
Benign"; "My dear, I had to seize the moment
And write. Can you still forgive me? Life is far
Too short for ten-year silences"—And even
The truths those messages encode: "You might as
Well come over"; "Cupcake, you're going wonky";
"The path report is grim"; "And by the way, I
Wonder if you could help me out with something"
Can never turn one against the cryptogram.
That code itself, the purest form of language,
Thrills the enciphering mind; putting the plain
Sense into travelling garb is a kind of
Singing. And until They change the codebook, my
Eleven seems a kind of measure fit for
Reaches of feeling as wide as any mode's
(Even hendecasyllabics, the darling
Of blatant, or of tenderer Catullus).
They could destroy this intimacy I have
Developed with my cipher, and every day
I await some frightful signal—a coughing
Caesura parting a phrase praising some foot
Preparation on the radio; a wrong
Addition on a bar check in my favor—
Letting me know that I must give it all up.
"All?" you'd ask—Well, I suppose not, but right now,
Reaching you in it, and without their knowing,
This code is all I have; my life is in your
Hands. Tomorrow change frequencies. Thine, Cupcake.

1/21

No report yesterday: a mechanical
Failure. I read the recent material
Sent on by Gland, and although in any case
It is of low grade, I have been wondering
About her going over: physical pain
Over a long period can give one back,
In detachment and patience, a mere fraction

7

Of what it takes away in joy. Her cover
Life has been battered in too many ways, too
Close to the work, and what with her grave problem
Of nationality to start with, it may
Be impossible to develop her case
Much further. But my evaluations are
Themselves in need of your evaluation;
And what with watching Artifact for any
Cracks, I wonder about my own detachment.
—This, of course, aside from wondering why I
Have been given this strange, complex assignment,
Playing through a medley of levels, when there
Is too much to do at any one of them.
I have been so fond of Gland. Do not trust her.

1/23

Report on Artifact: We met this morning
Beside the blue hippopotamus (faience,
Middle Kingdom). The man was quite visibly
Disturbed; he muttered of his children in the
South, and while he was passing on the exact
Location of the plant and the three places
The gas has been moved to, he kept glaring down
At his shoes as if his eyes were afraid to
Meet mine. Does he, by the way, have children
Notionally—or even actually?
I still have not pushed through to the depths of his
Cover, and indeed, to me (and to all the
Others, for that matter) he seems ill-suited
To his cloak of manifest life—We all find
It hard to live with the work, work with the life;
But some of us may have come to find a kind
Of homeliness therein, as in the cover
We take in our code-names: and some day, when I
Am recalled, and allowed leave in the mountains,
Looking across from some unclouded summit
To a distant, angular peak, white against

8

Blue, will I feel free of "cupcake"? Or, rather,
Stripped of it? Or is there perhaps a middle
Term of bareness, wanting but unencumbered?
(I will not speak of the joy we have in our
Names.) Tonight Artifact goes south for a week.

1/24

I have been studying Moroz, whose story
Is still being revived by various hands:
You know I have seen much of his file, followed
The life from here to London, the felonies
Of word by which he learned, having returned here,
To cover the work being done with muddling
Indirection, the terrors that felled all his
Family, the nearly saintly ruthlessness
He lived his cover with, while sucking dry the
Fountains he passed, poisoning many a well
He hoped that he would never need to draw from.
Covers of doubleness guard us for the work we
—I cannot say *do*, it is rather more like
Breathing than acting or making—but double
Covers, putting it out that he was low-grade
Personnel for the other side was, in its
Day, a bold and desperate thrust; and if it
Would seem like a child's game today, all whispers
And knocking down of chairs in excitement, it
Enabled him to continue longer than
Any of us could hope to do now. The Man
Moroz? Crueller than we are. The Moroz
Case? Inscribed in the Book of Work, O, and sealed.

1/24 (TO IMAGE)

Image, your cover alone has allowed you
Synoptic views of so many codebooks: have
You encountered European theories

Revealing the brotherhood of prophecy
And encipherment? I should have thought, rather,
That even the meanest cipher-clerk in an
Untroubled Embassy by some clear lake would
Be more of a voyeur, catching out his plain
Text unenveloped in her rough and outer
Layers of cloth—first peeled of these to lighter
Closenesses of veil, then still standing in her
Last rags of character, vanish behind the
Window-frame for a moment, suddenly to
Re-emerge, flesh-colored, in a nudity
Of inverted and erected digits mixed—
And glimpsing Truth when she looks so much like Love.
Then surely, stripped of ordinariness and
Openness to any eye, the enciphered
Text is lovelier and more mysterious
Than when obscured by layers of opaque sense.
Have you ever known anyone to run his
Thumb lovingly over a bill of lading
On which three abbreviations concluded
In fecund microdots? O Image, I have.

1/25

Reports keep coming in, other agents' work
For me to evaluate: you will by now have
Received the fresh material and I hope
I am wrong in feeling that no pattern
Has clearly emerged yet. It is hard enough
Merely to manage my own projects. Just this
Evening I left my desk for the window
To gaze out at the frozen river, winter
Sun flashing from the furrowed, gray ice,
And, squinting westward, realized that my day
Had been given over to "reading" blank sheets
Of ruled paper. What would active observers
Conclude from my motionlessness? What kind of
Work is it whose spent energy precedes by

So much time its glimpses of accomplishment—
Or indeed (worse, this) follows it. Which reminds
Me of something you should know: Artifact keeps
A photo of Felucca in his wallet.
I planned to drop in there tonight: I could drop
A kind of isotopic trace of fiction
(About shipments from the North, say?) into the
Tumbler of information as it were, then
Watch for it to surface, a rich pearl rising
Out of a dark cup of burgundy as it
Were, in Artifact's next transmission to you.
Is there some sound notional reason for the
Photo? Is there a story covering their
Friendship? O, quickly, quickly Lyrebird, fill me
In on this, or I soon must move against them.

1/25 (TO IMAGE)

What are we *doing*? The work goes on under
Cover of living, but when it—whatever
Part of it—is finished where will it be sealed?
Not in the shining Book of Life, but only
In the thick Book of Covers, whose promising
Leaves are all only specimen book-jackets,
Glossy or nobly stiff; garish; chaste; boastful;
Lettered only; or pictured; one of a series
Varying just in inscription or color—
A chamber of doors opening only on
Doors, whose opening closes off far more than
Walls can. A book neither of truth nor falseness.

1/26

I hope to have more soon about tactical
Uses of sound of the lowest frequencies.
Work must have been going on since that early
Incident in Montpellier eight years ago;

For so long nothing was suspected, because of
Childish beliefs, perhaps, in the power of
Signals inaudible because too high in
Frequency—singing ever unheard because
Unbearably above the human—to kill
Or madden or dissolve willing consciousness
(The shrill menaces: how can the quiet harm?).
Those first low rumblings, inaudibly torpid
(Four, five cycles per second of vibration)
Had consequences quite misunderstood at
The time—and, we hope, since. That dissolution
Could be generated by acts of nature
Wanting in excitation, too slow, too low
To be perceived, was more than escalating
Visions of destructiveness could engirdle.
There are two kinds of lowness in sound; this loud
Purring, like some pulse of the earth, is deep but
Strong. Of course They got on to it just about
When we did. Perhaps some poor simpleton, jarred
By an inner thunder never felt before
In a deep subway tunnel, put the two of
Under and rumble together with the two
Of visceral rubbing and then hemorrhage.
Perhaps he started to make inquiries and
Fell to his death before a breathless express.
Perhaps in Thumbtack's cover life he knew the
Dead man's sister—you see how it goes, and we
Have been developing the matter further
(Thumbtack is dull and rather reliable;
He may start asking for more money soon, though).
We will hope they have not gone too far with this.

1/27

Artifact, as you know, was broken early
Today, and as per instructions, Felucca
Monitored the tapes, which now leave no question

—You were, of course, right—and will have reached you by
The other route. Here I enclose a transcript
Of what our bug picked up from the listening
Felucca as she waited for him to come;
It is of no particular use to us.

(FELUCCA)
This waiting is worst. Everything is working—
Microphones in place, the hidden camera
Aimed at the bathroom medicine chest, almost
At the right bottle when the door is opened.
All is silent save for the sounds of midnight
Traffic outside, far below his apartment:
I hear them in my earphones as I wait here
In an adjoining dark flat for his return.
Turn, spool, turn, spool, spin, tape and wind him home now.

The tape recorder will be activated
By his footfall, which the shrewd machine knows as
Well as I do; then when he telephones them,
The flat, uncoiling serpent hissing softly
Will witness first his betrayal of the work.
Turn, spool, turn, spool, spin, tape and wind him home now.

They knew about us, gave me the assignment
Because of that, as if trapping a lover
Tested anything—as if everybody
I tailed or listened to or marked were not my
Man, all lovers were not on the Other side.
Turn, spool, turn, spool, spin, tape and wind him home now.

A greenish letter L eyes me from my watch.
Now there is a hiatus in the street noise.
My quietness is gone, my heart is heavy.
Turn, spool, turn, spool, spin, tape and wind him home now.

No, it was nothing: a traffic light must have
Changed, for the roar and hiss of trucks starting up

Unleashes once again the beasts of waiting.
Turn, spool, turn, spool, spin, tape and wind him home now.

The switch is off, untripped by any sounds of
Breathing even, the band of tape motionless
Save for when my finger heavily urges
The slow, reluctant take-up reel around. When
This is all over will they let me be done?
Turn, spool, turn, spool, spin, tape and wind him home now.

1/28

At sundown last week in a noisy, crowded
Cafeteria I caught two of Maisie's
People in conversation. Our equipment
Is now so good I could get all of it from
Halfway across the room. The two were Velvet,
An agent used for sabotage and bombings,
And old Hiccup, who mostly does decoding.
Lyrebird won't care about this much, but you might.

VELVET
Do well by the project. Nothing lies beyond
But madness, the incapacitating chill
Of madness. Who are "We"? Who "They"?—Neatly
Printed capitals at the heads of the ruled
Columns on my grandmother's bridge-scoring pads.
The names had for me as a child an order,
A mystery, quite apart from the way those
Curt pronouns were used in life. "We", then, and "They"—

HICCUP
Yes, We and They: and while we know who *They* are,
We must remember who we are as well, we
Who were at least taught to see that some problems
Were not just technical: "*Specta Teipsum*"

14

—"Each is an agent in the field of himself"—
So read the motto carved above the fire in
That panelled room in Cambridge where we were trained.
The work would be a game without the purpose.

VELVET
   The paired purposes—ours and theirs—are themselves
   Matched in a gimcrack tournament whose rules are
   Revised bi-monthly by a board of macaques.
   Do well by the project. Nothing lies beyond.

HICCUP
   But if you are right, we are those chattering
   Monkeys, playing the endless game that, meaning
   Nothing, standing for nothing but itself, casts
   Caravaggesque spotlighting on the sleazy
   Stage of "Purpose", making interchangeable
   Regions seem to be antithetical realms.
   And that they are so mocks your monkeyshines.

VELVET
   "We" and "They": The Eastern Theys, the Western We's,
   Two franchised teams play professional eyeball,
   And if we play well, where else is the good life?

HICCUP
   Beyond, beyond. Whatever world our cover
   Lives keep showing us pictures of, distorted
   But promising, this hope must be protected.

VELVET
   Purpose is sickening. The work would suffer.
   If there were justifications for it, how
   Could one bomb anything? or cause bystanders'
   Limbs to sail across the street, landing with a
   Wet thud at one's feet, if one were so fatuous
   As to feel that this price was paid for something.
   A clearly-broken, gaily emptied egg is
   All that the golden word *omelette* can mean.

HICCUP
You are afraid of gold, save for currency;
And speculation, save for the assignment's
Plot, you think a disease of the attention.
Even if we were to become like Them, then
We would at least know that opposing them had
Done that to us: we could go on opposing.

VELVET
History who would be your judge is hardly
Even a nightmare—it is something you ate.

HICCUP
You scorn the work even in doing it; at
Best, you will have been one of our utensils.

Their emptied glasses of tea cold before them,
They separated. The cafeteria's
Clatter dissolved the squawk of their pushed-in chairs,
And echoes flung the whole noise to the ceiling
With a tatty, starry sky painted on it.
I left, and walked outside where a streetlamp was
Flooding with first light an unwilling sidewalk.

1/29

We should have more soon from our political
People, although signs there are hardest to read.
There is no need to infiltrate the splinter
Parties, the professional wretches; and the
Parent Party of Hope suffers from loss of
Memory. Perhaps something might develop
With the newest Disembodiment movement,
But I am loath to advise it—their Public
Flaccidities, the sexual abstinence,
The craze for taking exotic placebos—
Sugar-pills, colored water, smoking cornsilk—

Fashionable now among older offspring
Of the false, hearty people . . . Not for us now.
This is a pupal stage of the heartiness
Preserved not through, but in, its damp and broken
Form, blossoming, coming to death in dry-furred
Wings, forever after fearing stickiness
And enclosure of just the sort a phase of
Itself exemplifies. It would be error
To interfere with one creature's life cycle.
If moth and worm were of two different species—
Ah, that might be another matter. Meanwhile
We shall keep to the usual fall of leaflets,
The broadcast sowing and the men of good will.

1/30

Strange, warm weather this week, a gentleness in
The January days tugging hard at the
Memory—Is this mild chill of vernal air
Recalled, or of fall? The threshold month's two old
Faces, back to back, look neither ahead and
Behind, nor (if one rotates the chart of the
Year through ninety degrees, to decipher it)
Above and below. No, they look in and out.
Rooting out the blossom of one's response to
This mad attenuation of the cold calls
For following a line of inner gaze deep
Enough to hit spring, or, with a shallower
Look, to come to rest in the recent autumn.
The outward look? That is our constant, working
Wariness. But I digress. The vast report
Compiled by Riddle on the recent uses
Of belief has raised eyebrows but no searching
Questions—all the other agencies have let
It drop; our people will have to deal with it.
Has this warm air affected my transmissions?

No word in the press of Artifact's body.
On the job (cover) today, wandering down
High corridors, past shadowed glass cases,
I caught a darkened glimpse of myself, moving
Against a background of uninteresting
And broken red-figured pots, and wondered
What this careful and reticent career would
Be without the work to do beneath its
Brisk palimpsest: it would be in a way still
Life; my face dim among fractured kraters can
Remain as it is no more than a shard of
An entire figure, pieces of which were in
Berlin, and some perhaps in London as well.
I ran to my office and the welcoming
Bright grays of my own world of prints, their hard light
And reliable parts of dark, and welcomed
The daily tasks, acknowledging the bequests—
For there are continual bequests—and then
I wondered what I will be permitted to
Acquire, and whether the work makes me better
Or worse at this job I fill a false self with.
But that false self reflects back a real image.
I know that I am surrounded with light, too,
By watching the black kitty's eyes, all yellow
Around pinpoints of darkness, turning toward me.

2/1 (TO IMAGE)

Image, there were funny pings in my headset
During the transmission tonight, echoing
Neither in my head nor in the earphone, but
Somewhere within, it seemed to me, their own sound.
Transmitting the truth is always a problem.
Facts we can encipher, and they then become
Sendable messages: why do not the truths

Climb obediently into disguises,
Learn their lines well and be off? Instead they hang
About and plague us with unvoiced reproaches.
Perhaps these headset pings—I dreamt last night I
Fled someone, and ran into a cave ("This is
A place of broken artifacts" rang in my
Ear as if I had just been so instructed);
Then I was sitting down and heavy pebbles
Were dropping around me at slow intervals
("Broken echoes" my head said). Then I awoke,
Forgetting the dream, the cave, the broken stones.
Tonight the dying sounds inside my headset
Recalled them all. Echoes of truth? Collect them,
Image, fragmentary as they are, like shards
Of mirror, each of them reflecting the whole.

2/4

No transmissions for the last two days, while we
Shifted our frequencies. Kidd has been in touch
—To no consequence, but it may develop.
In the matter of Artifact—and am I
Already thinking of it as history?—
There is so little, finally, to be said:
As always, we all made errors, and there were
Accidents—the cancelled flight, the illness of
A principal dancer that Sunday evening—
And finally, the big mistake, and the wrong
Letter left about, the tiny rip along
One seam of the cover and that was the end.
The case of Artifact was developed so
Beautifully just from that splendid yardage,
As it were, of cover. But things open up.
And as always we must console ourselves here
With knowing that after that point neither you
Nor we had any choice ("No case is ever
Finished, but only abandoned." Remember?)

2/4 (TO IMAGE)

Your crocus has reported, its cups aflame.
The two cats, if you take my meaning, are quite
Perplexed—there are none of the usual leaves
To nibble: one can almost believe they feel
The dark power of all that early burning,
The promises, albeit indoors, of earth.
Fancy—the outcry of earth in a small pot
Enciphered, in an apartment. *Il Grido*
Della Terra—terrible return of spring—
This will be the password for the coming weeks.

2/5

The unlucky Felucca acknowledges
Receipt, she says, of her new instructions. I
Wonder less about what they are, than what she
Herself must think about what disposition
Will be made of her case: this will interfere
With the quality of any work she does
For me, or for others. Is it permitted
To wonder about this? (Heading the list of
Forbidden questions is "What are the contents
Of that list itself?" I know) Imagining
What must be on it, I have long considered
What problem, if I were to go wrong, would set
Me brooding: not "Am I trusted?"—trust, as we
Know, is only one of many biases;
"Am I useful?"—the question is always
"How?"; but "What has the work, in the end, revealed?"
—A good load of tidings, heavy with sweet news,
Needing two strong men to bear back with them? or
Bad news for our side, that among the people
Of this land we can hope for nothing?—news which
Even we, the unwitting bearers of, must
Somehow now be feeling to be burdensome.

So many of the old agents say they seem
To themselves, toward the end of afternoon,
Like small, dust-colored grasshoppers unable
To budge. Is it permitted to wonder why?

2/6 (TO IMAGE)

We who have done work on the Final Cipher
Know both how near and how far we always are,
When using the routine codes for the mundane
Messages, from stumbling over even one
Of its principles by which the principles
Of a finite cipher were made to vary.
Knowing this much means that we know how little
We can know. But I have been considering
A cipher lying outside the wide range of
All our contingent codings, but providing
A limiting case for the spectrum—and no,
I do not mean plain text itself, uncoded,
As the "ultraviolet" cipher, but its
"Infrared" perhaps—the five-letter groups which
Cannot be decoded in any manner
Because there is no text embedded in them.
A limiting case—but one authenticating,
In a mad kind of way, the grades of what we
Call "difficulty" in the ciphers of life.
Are there other such cases—not only of
Encodings, but of reassuring limit?
Thus: the one case of metastatic despair
Whose treatment of choice would have the doctor lie
With the patient; the clearly indicated
Suicide; or, in our sad terms, the one case
Of an agent sent out, maintained at great cost
With the intention that he go bad, perhaps
Even go over, shaking up a good deal
Of what had been built up over the long years,
But—and this is most crucial—*to no purpose.*
Do we not need to know that once, and somewhere,
This had been done, and, indeed, that it was right?

2/6

Very well then: no more of what you call my
Blithering. Felucca remains steady and
Maisie requires, he says, a new frequency—
The old one is hemmed in by overloaded
Neighboring ones. The work on all aspects of
Project Lamplight, in its solitary way,
Continues: May I only be in on its
Completion: may any of us only be.

2/9

There have been no transmissions. Power lines are
Down, airports snowed in, the whole city asleep
This morning beneath bright snow, wildly gleaming
In a bare hour of sun, patted into smooth
Shape by windy nixies of the after-storm.
Last night, Tallman and I met in a vast and
Nearly empty part of a new aerodrome
And were stranded for hours there at the edge
Of the city. Today we contrived to get
A plane out and I hope we shall have finished
Taking care of these loose ends in the matter
Of Steampump by tomorrow. But even now
The weather here is deteriorating
And we have discovered a nest of agents
Of various sorts who seem to have converged
On where we are this weekend. The snow drifts
Seem to get visibly higher outside and
The wind whines hopelessly as if trying
To reach a clear frequency it might speak on.
I hope we can get out of here. I hope this
Reaches you by these most unusual means.

2/13

I am acting under the old instructions
Still, having heard nothing new from you. I am
On my way to meet Tallman in another

City, flying as I am wont to do with
My gaze pressed up against the window. From it
The available world down and out, reduced
To a strategic map of itself seems so
Vulnerable, more so than the most frail bird
Bearing my eye aloft; but that map over
Which I have ever delighted to pore reads
Always as the most nagging kind of puzzle.
Whether shaded in with June greens and the yellow
Of old roads, or hiding cloudily under
Whitish blurs—the bruised gray of February,
Its black smudges—the same enigma remains:
While we may know just what the map is of, what
Is it *for*? What sinews of the living land
Are charted there? What modes of life are coded
By green and yellow? What wild hues are reduced
To black and white? What does this map envelop?
Tallman, pretending he does not know me, sits
In the seat up ahead; he gazes down at
Pictures, not maps. Cloudscapes are what he sees from
Far above, far fields of rich cloudland blending
At the edges of sight with distant waters
Almost audible: these are all the landscapes
Left, the yet unpainted scenes that his eye can
Hold without the intervening spectacles
Of finished pictures anciently brushed into
Place, of the twilight of darkening varnish.
I have my maps. We shall see what they are for.

2/18

Still no report from you. I have returned from
All trips for the time being. Tallman has left
The country. I went out last night and looked in
The usual places for emergency
Messages—there were none—and gloomily I
Considered how the unclouded winter night,
The mad kakeidoscope of unspinning stars

23

And shiftings only of darkness in between,
Whatever they meant, could mean no good even
For us, our lives, or for what work may be left
For us—and gloomily I hoped for some high,
Mercurial wind to brush up half-pearled clouds
Over the hopelessness of such clarity.
Best, on such nights, that no messages reach me.

2/19 (TO IMAGE)

The project relevant to which I enclose
Some material that you have already
Seen was abandoned three years ago and now,
Its cover long since blown, can be, as it were,
"Published"—these reports as you see, represent
The best work we can do. But situations
Melt and flow and fill other possible forms,
One of their people gets called to another
City, planetary configurations
Shift, the average rainfall in October
Is down—so much that we can wonder just what
Former projects were for. And if the very
Work itself did not yield up new unworked fields,
Then the work itself would so change in time that
Older maps would look quaint, tables add up right
Only with some new number base, cross-sections
Read as decorative doodles—We would have
To get on with it again in any case.
And in any case, this one now, for your files.

2/20 (TO IMAGE)

In re the Final Cipher again: it would
Have to hold this invariant property,
That any unsuitable message—falsehoods,
Mistakes of transmission, bungled assignments
Yielding ore of too low a grade, and high truths

Employed in some nevertheless doubled way
To trap us with—all these would simply not fit
The code, and go into it as cipher which
Decoded would unlock only gibberish—
Like a language in which all lies came out in
Ungrammatical sentences, or way of
Water color in which all uglinesses
Ran and blotted even the fair neighboring
Parts whose beauty nastier ones would enhance.
Could this be built into the code alone?

2/20

Kidd has, I have been able to determine,
Received instructions from you while I still wait
For word. Kidd came, as you may gather, up to
The museum today ostensibly in
Re the Rembrandt etching (Hind 260, Bartsch
270—a yet-unrecorded state),
But actually, I think, to let me know
You were running him directly. This is not
Good; but as always I assume that
Lyrebird knows what he is doing. Kidd told me
That you had told him that you hoped he could take
Comfort from his work. I assume that you would
Never insult my understanding by such
A suggestion: The work is like—what for most
People is life itself. Our life—the layers of
Cover, for me the museum, for Kidd the
Career of arrangements—is what we labor to
Maintain. Kidd seemed pleased. Unless you have further
Comments, Project Red and Project Blue now stand
As they are. Orange will perhaps come next, but
Not yet. I cannot develop Orange yet.

2/21

A bad dream: I am sitting on a daybed
Looking at an unlit lamp in the corner
When a crowd ("of accusers" I hear inside

My head) begins to fill the room, and I can
Make out the faces of Pike and Prettyboy
And, sidling up behind them, Gland, and I know
With that dreaming a priori certainty
That I know the others as well; a voice tells
Me that I am feeling the presences of
The Dead, and indeed I experience a
Physical pressure exerted by the space
I am dreaming of, and in. But Gland is not
Dead, and Prettyboy has been seen hereabouts,
And Pike seems to have been reporting in: Why
These? Was I as dead, menaced by the shades of
The living? Is it merely that I do not
Trust them utterly? Of what am I afraid?
(For Lyrebird: are the instructions still the same?)

2/27

I have remained silent for some days, leaving
The frequency open, hoping to catch out
Some of the false reports that you may have been
Getting among my own. You will have to change
The schedule of drops—I have not heard from you
Just at the needed times, and I have only
Low-grade information about these reports.
In any event, if you were sent something
In plain text about Minoan Pottery,
Or about butterflies near a general's
Tomb, or a long account of (can this be right?)
Bee-keeping in the south, do not, repeat, do
Not attempt to puzzle it all out. There is
Nothing: this is no matter of notional
People—families, employers—or places
Of business or pleasure. No, these are fictions,
Some madman is introducing fictions where
There can be only truths or the lies with which
We gather our sheaves of truth, leaving gleanings
Of dead straw for Their side. These reports are too

26

Interesting to be mine—all I have sent
You has been dull. I am a dull fellow. We
Must remove this nuisance: please check with sources
And find out if Their people have been troubled
Similarly. Perhaps we can work with them
On this. The cipher still seems quite secure, though.
Please advise on the matter of the fictions.

2/27 (TO IMAGE)

A bad bleak week, with the work as usual
Confined to boring transmissions whose value,
Locked up inside the details of tedium,
We are never to know; and it depresses
Me even more to realize how very
Much depends on these exchanges with you. A
Clear night, an available unmonitored
Frequency, a saved-up note or two, the first
Dear crackle of static—it is not that I
Prize them (and this is dangerous) for themselves,
But for the activity they provide a
Fabric for: our little thoughts on the nature
Of code. The work, I know, is fragile—and to
Celebrate even the small part of it that
Ciphering is, is thereby a weakening.
But when our eyes are sealed from any ends save
For the End itself, that scrimmage of We and
They, what then could be left us other than to
Brood over the codes, praise the means that the means
So coldly uses. Their beauty, the ciphers?
O, I suppose we have been left with that, too,
Harmless as a kind of humming while we work.

2/28 (TO IMAGE)

One prefers not to remember too clearly
The day of one's recruitment; but you must have
Felt, as I did, that getting a code name was
More compelling than any mission, even
Than what one might have then imagined the work

To be. As I stood invisibly wrestling
With my recruiter by the river on an
April evening, I realized all at
Once that my decision was already made
When he said *"Cupcake.* That is how even now
You are listed among the possibles," and
Just then my name—not the cover one, sleazy
In its ingenious plausibility, but
The one that might be inscribed and sealed somewhere—
Rang in my heart as a foghorn brayed along
The water. Names like ours leave no traces in
Nature. Yet what of the names they encode, names
One's face comes in time to rhyme with, John or James?
The secret coded poem of one's whole life rhymes
Entirely with that face, a maddening
Canzona, every line of which sings in the
Breaths we take and give, ending with the same sound.
As with the life, so ridiculously, with
The work. But, after all, which of them is the
Enciphered version of the other one, and
Are we, after all, even supposed to know?

3/1

All quiet here. Again, no report from you.
Scattered outbreaks of terror do not abate.
I have been concluding that our lives, fulfilled
As they are by the work (so we must believe)
Are uniquely free of terror. Terror is
The condition in which we are disabled
From doing what we must, and know we must, do,
And, with a preparatory contraction
Of will, choose violently to do what
Will help to breed more terror everywhere,
The ransom paid, the agent forced to double,
The dear friend abandoned because the arrows
Of madness lie beyond a young courier.
And for even the most free of multitudes
The instruments of torture are always on

General exhibition, but we with no
Freedom are immune, we who have no people
To be taken hostage, nothing to betray
Save a few ciphers, a minor agent or
Two, a frequency about to be changed in
Any case. Thus the work evaporates on
Our exposure to air, and we are always
Enabled to do what must be done. Violence?
Danger? The presence of death? Yes—but safety
From the terror which only the illusion
Of freedom arms, informs and helps to finance.

3/2

Your transmission of yesterday received and
Now being processed. You should by now have seen
Two copies of the papers relating to
Project Lilith, long since, of course, abandoned.
Since hearing from you I can now reassure
Some of the agents, strung out along the chain
Of crazy discourse not so much connecting
Them as running through them, that all present plans
Indeed continue. But this anxiety
About not having heard is trivial: what
Concerns me more for all of them occurs in
Tiny moments in the midst of things—as when
The coding of some message will not go right
And one stares at the cipher text and the stuffed
Paper shredder for much too long. Or when in
A bad stage of something—torturing someone
To make him reveal where one of our people
Is being tortured though we know nearby—the
Impossibility of going on lights
Up a bright spinning firmament of other
Possibilities. But then, mercifully,
The closure comes, not darkness overtaking
The pale stars ranged in front of it, but a gray
Solvent for light and dark both, and multitudes
Of starry alternatives become merely

The silent heartbeats of the multitudes of
Others. They are not possible for one at
All. And so one is enabled at the end
To get on with it; still these are the moments
I fear most. I always fear for all of us.

3/8 (TO IMAGE)

Your moving memoir of those uncompleted
Investigations, the splendidly designed
But not fully executable projects—
Ungarlanded flowers, in a sense, they are
Jeunes filles en fleurs—or Feuilles Jaunes,
As older service people still will call them—
Beautifully and sadly suggests once more
How so many volumes, after all, of the
Book of oneself lack the true thread, are merely
Florilegia plucked of the time, posy
Anthologies rather than a collection
Of Works: deeds which are truly not enough our
Doing, acts about which the lame excuses
We send back ("No one could have foreseen how . . ."
"The agent just went bad on us" "The weather . . .")
Do not, indeed, say false things as excuses
So often do. But on your pages even
The dimmed candor of light less than white reveals
What smudges all our shadows, in yellowing
Leaves that drop to the ground where winter ever
Remains. And yours, giving such light, hang bravely
In the old wind, flowers of enduringness
And, even with the most fragile, of themselves.

4/3 (TO IMAGE)

Today in doing some routine decoding
I thought, as a sad, mild wind brushed with half a
Heart at the papers on my desk, of the days
When no decoding was routine, when ciphers

All gleamed with newness and possibility.
Even the dully reliable British
Playfair we sent our schoolboy messages in
Was like an epic line we had mastered; and
The elementary polyalphabets
We sported with, the few hopefully simple
Columnar transpositions were our wit, our
Triolets of encipherment, our rondeaux
Of encoding. O, how all the bright schoolboys
Darken, their earnest games chilling into life!
Our grammars mapped the inexorable; we
Knew then what sequence of moods showed the future
More vivid; we splashed, callow, over the deep
Pool of language in which only swimmers drown.
We must not forget. We must keep asking for
Ciphers more difficult, each month, to use, lest
Our care and hope vanish into the message,
Coding having become too much a matter
Of sighing, flopping into one's chair, reaching
Wearily for the new grid of the week, and
Starting with the calculations. The noisome
Flutter of papers, like a flick of fear brought
By an unwitting wind, would be too welcome.
The need for *frissons*—that is most dangerous,
The void in which our people often vanish.

4/6

Resuming regular reports: the recent
Trip went as planned; the information gathered
Is being enciphered now and will reach you
In good time. Kidd may be getting greedy: but
Perhaps we need a new paymaster here in
Any case. Cram broods a lot. I did not get
To make contact with Riddle. Nowhere I went
Was there word to be heard of Lac, and for all
Practical purposes the stuff he sends them
Is of such low grade as to be even worse
Than useless (and you know well how much Lac used

To count with them). But more of that later.
The cover museum visit went well too;
And at one drop—the last one—I acquired a
Surprising batch of etchings. Well, then: normal,
Profitable and safe, and for a bonus
The memory of one great monument I
Had never seen before, a gleaming structure
Of such high, open scale, looping through such a
Pool of sky, that I was quite astonished by
My own capacity to be astonished—
At something not unruined and not of stone—
Still, after all—after all that and all this.

4/7

My memory may be going, in the way
Of little pieces of detail that—like the
Face, the chimney, half the carriage wheel, on their
Squiggles of jigsaw puzzle piece laid aside
And then groped for helplessly—will not come. They
Leave only hard-edged blanks which look exactly
Like so many others similarly cut
Where the name—and it is usually a
Name—should be. This all may, peculiarly
Enough, affect cover activities more
Than the work itself. But it will come, I should
Think, in its turn, even though so much consists,
Now, in the transmissions of current affairs.
Just today I was unable to recall
The name of one of the museum's best print
Suppliers in Amsterdam—my visitor
Thought I was being devious about the
Provenance of an engraving: what kind of
Intrigue must he ascribe to my unspotted
Covering life! There are tasks for which, perhaps,
Freedom from memory would be a blessing,
And yet the laughter of nine anonymous
Girls in some loudly marble public hall would

Always await one. Tell Lyrebird I am well
For the moment. I still await his visit.

4/10

Nothing more than routine reports from any
Of the agents. As for your last suggestion,
I must say that I feel strongly negative—
Microdots in the catalogues from Brussels
Are technically simple enough, and I
Don't say that a fine impression of, say, "The
Hundred Guilder Print" offered to us at the
Prevailing ludicrous prices will seem too
Insecure for the precious period that
Brings " . . . in splendid condition." to a full stop.
No: keep the museum thing out of it for
Now at any rate. Aunt Clara will still serve.
Cover and work must embrace without touching—
Too crude an intrusion of either into
The other endangers the security
Of both. Either way, bad, then. Bad for the work.

4/16

No news yet. I hear that one of Their people
(Flypaper, I believe) has tried to run off
—Not to us, certainly (and where else is there,
After all, to go?) Poor wretch: it is not as
If he had really ever aspired to much.
"The length of things is vanity, only their
Height is joy" (this, from some lecture long ago
On air reconnaissance, I still remember).
But what are we all, who even coming up
For air from below ground are thereby soaring?
And when it finally comes to flight even
Birds return to beastliness; their crowns ahead,
No longer atop, quivering ziggurats

33

Collapsed, their minor verticality was
Never the perilous condition of our
Being upright, even in a land of hills.
Flight is safe. Standing is what we dare to do.
By next week Flypaper will have been shot down.

4/17

Enclosed you will find the requested reports
On available mental institutions
In this part of the country. I have made all
The usual payments and picked up something
Of other groups. It all adds up as you might
Expect to this: Lac grows daily more tiresome;
Funding him by now must be an enormous
Burden for whomever is running him, and
What he brings in will never be any good.
He seems obsessed with his place in histories
Of intelligence. It would be a kindness
To other people working in the field to
Terminate his case; but who is ever shown
A kindness, in the work? By the way, all that
I gather from sources indicates that Lake,
As always, continues to be trustworthy,
And our most valuable of people, cold
As she is, gray, and unlike Lac, unruffled.
I hope that in a crisis we should never
Have to end her work merely that his should cease.

4/18 (TO IMAGE)

These nights of ciphering, Image, can be quite
Sickening: long stretches of intensity
Without the quickening excitement which comes
With decipherment, and then nausea at dawn
When its grey weight of mere labor accomplished
Settles in all the corners of the room where

34

The taut lamplight has not been reaching all night.
It is as if one had been drained of something
Like light. And after, say, six working nights of
Fashioning cryptograms one would want to be
Able to look upon his literal world
Half-forgetting what it enciphered; one would
Want to walk one's gaze among the cool columns
Of letter groups, through the shades of averted
Signification. That would be the one world
Where letter itself was all the spirit that
Was, where there was no need for withdrawals
Into the dark of trope, nor for the builded
Eidolon of piled-up pebbles, the one world
Whose anatomy would be an enciphered
Text of itself, the one world best left in plain.
That would be the world where we were unneeded.

4/30

In case tonight's contact fails to occur, I
Transmit the following for the attention
Of Lyrebird: Last night I picked up, enciphered
The usual way, and on the previous
Week's frequency, a scrap of puzzling message:
THE RED SHIP IS CREATED—and I had the
Feeling that this not only had concluded
Some report, but that, as a clause, somehow it
Was contrastive, that there had been something on
The one hand [. . . (BUT) THE RED SHIP] etcetera.
But what contrasted with—something that evolved?
Something already there? Imaginary?
As I closed up the transmitter and hid its
Workings as usual in the wall behind
Piranesi's cut boulders and unbroken
Chains, possibilities of that floating phrase
Fanned out like a pale wake in clouded moonlight—
It was as if I had awakened from light
Sleep with the words still bubbling at my lips, while

Critical daylight defined a dry shore on
Which I lay, breathless, against hard pebbles.
In view of everything, I thought that Lyrebird
Should know what little there is to know of this.

4/30 (TO IMAGE)

Image: I could not reach you before you left
And so shall send this on to be picked up at
The Athens drop—I gather you flew off this
Evening, at the sharp angle of ascent to
Which we have become inured, and flying east
At evening, with the promise of outrunning
Darkness (memories of twilight reflected
On the wings' trailing edges, while the gleam of
False morning winks along the leading ones) is
So wearying a suspension. Not as it
Once was, in the slow times of the great steamers—
Nine-day crossings on smaller ships; time to try
The new cover life on for size, stretching its
Youth; flowers at parting, scents soon to be
Assaulted by the rinsing sting of the brine;
Wireless news; and always the hope for some young
Person from Smyrna and a quiet passage
Of surfaces. But that is not how you left.
Take these lines as a delayed posy, or more
Properly, for one of those elevenses
In the gulf stream, high sunlight gleaming in the
Heart of the tea; wrapped in cover, one waited
For the grounded deceptions of the new shore.

5/1 (TO IMAGE)

Look, Image, at one aspect of the work's long
History which has taken my especial
Attention—I mean the name of our species
Of speculation (as from standing on the

High *specula*, or "watchtower", to extend
The normal scope of sight into the alleys
Of enemy tents, one expects). The common
Root of all our words specifically of
Looking, some hypothetical *spek*-like word,
Spoken past dim antiquity once, spawned our
Name—*spy*—that of a seeker, not a seer,
Then (through some auspiciously intervening
Spectral ancestor word form, some barbaric
Spehon, or *spion* or the like) ending up
With us, skeptical in all our unwisdom,
We, the specious: our names and natures descend
From the Romance, down to the despicable
Monosyllable of our lot. Inspect, thus,
Like some Temple of Vision's frontispiece, its
Many-eyed façade, through time's logoscope, our
Common name—ours and theirs, in Conflict's despite.

5/9

The major work on project Aspasia
Is now complete and full reports are being
Prepared. It took time, but as you might conclude,
The Lady could not be hurried along. I
Have heard little from the others: the wretched
Gland will be out of town for a bit, Riddle
Waits for things to develop, Kidd is silent
(At least, to me: I'm sure he is off being
Noisy somewhere). A strange thing, though: yesterday
I got through ordinary mail a moving letter
From Puritan (you remember what once in
Venice the fading Kilo on his pale bed
Said when I told him Puritan, sending his
Regards, "wished to be remembered"?—Kilo half
Looked up: "He is in no danger of being
Forgotten" was the reply—I still don't know
Whether charming or gaga—*that* Puritan).
I would echo Kilo here. And as we all

Shrink from general notice, pruning back our
Covers to be better shaded by them, we
Must keep our own annals illuminated
All the more fully. Puritan, no longer
In the service, yet can hardly not be said
To be involved with the work still, and always.

5/10 (TO IMAGE)

To come, Image, upon the Final Cipher,
Perhaps to see it gradually take shape
Under the doodling and fussing of an hour
Of idleness, the while a pressing message
Remains, uncoded in its naked plain on
The desk by one's left hand—this would be something
Given indeed. Neither growing beneath the
Transmission's heavy demands, nor with the false
Spontaneity of what arises in
Play—perhaps thus not taken, grasped, wheedled
Out of the Sibyl of Codes. Truly given.
Then, being available, its use would be
Inevitable: one would come to discern
The world—even the innocent, unworking
World—in it, would somehow walk in its rhythms
Of transposition, in its modes of shifting.
The perfect cipher: effortless to handle
By the instructed, and yet impossible
To misuse. For all the others? So patent,
So transparent as not to be there at all,
Drowning them in the pool of plain text, losing
Them, and their wits, in excessive clarity.
A poem whose form was of the world itself.

5/11

The results of the last few days will surely
Bring Lyrebird no joy, but that cannot be helped.

Political deteriorations have
Brought other structures down as well, the fabric
Of many walls has been ripped, and our cover
Clawed away at in many places—one of
Our banks, as you will have discovered, is in
Danger, and among the agents, even Kidd
Is losing his credit rapidly, and may
Have to be shifted into something harmless.
And I? Despair, as you know, for the future
Of Project Orange—it still goes so slowly—
And, even worse, growing lack of conviction
About its value for the work: Their Project
White is so protean an enterprise that
Our bits and pieces of counter-strategy
Can only chip away at bits of what They
Are constantly at work at. It is almost
As if that operation of Theirs were part
Of nature, that in trying to cope with it,
Building and unbuilding our sorry models,
Annihilating the appearances to
Reach the workings behind them, we were engaged
In something that we had not contracted for.
White is too large a matter to be thought of
As an operation, even. And my poor
Little Orange now, hopefully projected?
—You must feel some of this unease yourself. At
Least, all is untroubled at the Museum.
A shipment of bronzes arrives tomorrow.

5/12

Urgent to Lyrebird: do They have one of Their
People at the Museum too? Check on this.
Today at the Acquisition Meeting one,
Of the new bronzes caught my eye—a splendid
Aphrodite whapping Pan with her sandal—
And something in the provenance seemed strange, with
An early attribution "Claus of Innsbruck".

Clearly a signal (perhaps a cipher key)—
At any rate, too crude for any of our
People to use (and I would have thought any
Of Theirs). I do not like this much. Please advise.

5/12 (TO IMAGE)

We are plain, Image, to ourselves even when
Reversed in our mirrors; but to others are
We like cipher letters?—One hopes not. One wants
To be a kind of null, a meaningless but
Hopefully confusing figure strewn about
Among the truly ciphering characters
Of a secret message—an X standing for
No kiss even, yet alone a plain letter.
Thus, to the simple ones to whom there are no
Puzzles, we pass among the rest of things, to
The others who read everything as cipher,
We are to be disregarded as meaning
Nothing. So would we be safe. Consider the
Case of an agent with no cover life at
All, but who would appear to disappear when
Not working on an assignment, an agent
Whose only life was as a part of the work.
He would be a pure null. Yet in another
Sense, we have nulls: The Foot, Maisie, Felucca,
The late Artifact, Thumbtack, Hiccup, Velvet,
Flypaper—and for all I am ever to
Know, Lyrebird him-or herself—standing among
The cipher letters of our kind, unkeyed to
Any text of life to be derived from theirs:
Notional characters, thinner than fictions,
Yet fully formed on these pages they dwell in.

5/13

While compiling the figures you requested
I saw Ember today at the Museum.
He has grown astonishingly beautiful
In the past few years as the high quality
Of the work he does for us has become more
Apparent. Is it something in his cover—
Something that builds character where only a
Personality is called for? Or has he
Secretly revealed himself to take drink of
A sweet and demanding source? That would be bad:
He would be found out all too quickly. But he
Looks too well—it is as if the work itself
Were Nourishing him now. How he has risen
From the old ashes of himself! I recall
His former crabbed privacies, his sad, fussy
Insistence on obscure French restaurants at
Noon for passing messages, the bizarre keys
For ciphers he would invent. Now he seems an
Illumination of the ordinary,
An image swept up from among uncials.
It is as if his work were of the wide world,
That "universal and public manuscript."

5/14

You will have received by now the new reports
On submarine developments, corrected
For the most recent policy decisions.
Shall I proceed further there, or try to get
Project Orange launched at last? Although there is
Nothing manifestly relating them, I
Cannot help feeling that the undersea things
Affect the shiningly surface matters of
Orange, and thereby all the other facets
Of Project Lamplight, more than we had ever
Imagined. I await your advice on this.

Meanwhile, the matter of security at
The Museum has been settled: the "Claus of
Innsbruck" thing was, fortunately, only a
Prank (of the Museum's—as it were—"agent"
In Basle; and I am told the bronze itself
Was not at all right). All is well, then. Nothing
Of this affects the work (although the prank is
The sort of thing Kidd used to do in some of
His most important reports, but never since
He has been working with us, naturally).
My budget there has been cut back, but that is
Just part of a wide general retrenchment.

5/15

Inquiries that you suggested be made in
Regard to Kidd yield little—he has not been
Seen for some weeks (at any rate, by any
Of the couriers that I inquired among).
But he will surface, soon enough, bobbing up,
If not like a homely reliable old
Cork, then like a gaily-painted float, although
The trouble with Kidd is not the work he does,
But with—how can I put it?—the style with which
He lives his cover, liking too much the wrong
Things about it, while yet despising the one
Element he most needs to trust: himself. He
Sells himself far too cheaply, like some former
Tart, long since a countess, slipping out at night,
Going up to town to take on a few louts
(Not for their brawn—they are seedy and nervous)
For twopenny uprights in a public park—
As if to reassure herself of her near-
Worthlessness. So with Kidd. Having made the grand
Sale of one's life, one should rejoice in the high
Price, in its fairness, as a blossoming of
Worth. Kidd's world of Arjay Enterprises may
Remain good working cover, but the air in

There, as it were, is bad. It cannot be good
For him, for his part of the work, for us all.

6/1 (TO IMAGE)

I have been working around the clock at some
Museum things, and there has been little chance
To get a message out to you. Today I
Went walking in the park where a clear, mute wind
Blew from tall buildings encircling the dancing
Grass, and I felt a clarity then, and then
A loss; and it was not until I came out
On a street of glittering boutiques crowded
With pleasant strangers that I was given a
Sign (not those wonders on the shops: "ET LES GANTS"
Across the avenue, "THE VENERABLE
BEAD"—M.'s place—or, in a window, a menu
Featuring FETA COMPLI—Decay lunches
There—and two doors further down a great onyx
"J"—for JIMMY'S—with a silver "B" below)
No, signs: half-glimpses in wide, dark half-mirrors
Of shop window, behind one, a large antique
Mirror, half-registering in the eye, half-
Retreating from it. Then I remembered
—With a shock of knowing that these were not of
My eye entire, but of half-surfaces—
How much I had missed our little messages.
As you can see, I have resumed the same old
Frequency. Is all distinct again? All clear?

6/6

Your unexpected visit of last week was
Most helpful, and letting it get about that
You had come down yourself has allowed many
Of our people to firm up their groups—although
Kidd, I gather, still remains out of contact.

I hope he is not ill, nor that he has gone
Over: but you will doubtless know about this.
The work on Project Orange has been halted:
I know its import for the whole of Lamplight,
But reaching the point of no return on things
Like this is no matter of merely turning
A switch and then letting what will be be,
But more like fussing with a damp tinder-box
That one had never been taught to use, in a
Play that was slipping, with the rapidity
Of dream, around the high proscenium which
Framed off the fictions from the bare walls of fact.
Perhaps when the weather is right we might try
Again. Perhaps you will visit before then.
I will in any case put Kidd out of mind.

6/10 (TO IMAGE)

Your having picked up the last message noted
With satisfaction as also comprising
A sign of your return—I keep saying "sign"
As if those hideous counter-examples
Of nonsignification that I mentioned
Half-frivolously in my last message had
Still some unfinished business with me. Last night
I know I dreamed disturbingly of being
Among a forest of such signs: ice dripped from
HOCH AND SELTZER, RESTORERS as suddenly
I was with a crowd of many in a warm
Wooden inn (someone said "the Anglo-Norman
Place", and I thought first of manuscripts, running
Through narrow corridors, looking at framed things
On walls); then I ran out the door in terror
Lest I see the broad signboard overhead, swung
Out at a mad angle and frozen there and
Lest I read the dreaded name there: FRIAR TOQUE—
I awoke, mercifully, with pounding heart.
Clearly, unread or rejected signs given

Us, will have their own back—and yet how can we.
Even in the work, consider everything?
Is there not anything that has not been left
There by someone as a sign for someone else?
When seen out of the corner of one's glance, two
Sticks in the mud, a piece of trampled candy
Wrapper—these bore through the eye of augury.
But viewed directly, the clear, frank, random grass,
The leaves of some unwanted circular, all
Seem purged of intention, seem not set there, but
Merely given. What part of one's eye lies, then?

6/15 (TO BUN)

This should not go out on this frequency, but
It is all I have now to send on and I
Hope that none of them will be listening at
This hour. Just to say, then, that when high over
The city at sundown—buildings becoming
Blocks of immense darkness through which shone all their
Local stars, slow lines of light crawling along
The riverbank—I waited for a moment
Amid the windiness that hid not even
Whispers, amid the insistences of chill:
I remembered it all. Not as points, corners
Or even lit or dark streets, straight or crooked,
But all, unrolled below like all the shining
Island, stretched south and east and west—there was no
View to the dread north. I knew, remembering,
That what I had forgotten you would have—as
Always—remembered. Now in the long darkness
Marked not by shiftings of the light nor changes
Of cloud, but by the unseen, general stars,
I glance up at the clocked hour remembering
All the things. I need not try to list them yet.

6/16 (TO GRUSHA)

To Grusha, on the instructions of Lyrebird:
A warm day. Orange continues to smolder

45

Without erupting into action. Meanwhile,
As per your last suggestion we have commenced
Surveillance of The Foot. Though there has been some
Grumbling, I personally do not mind long
Hours of night observation: staring out of
The darkness into light. That is the vital
Part of it—rather than the excitment of
Waiting for movement to violate the sharp
Composure of a picture, or the early
Moment when the first focussing twirl of knob
Brings a bright blur of—(what? sense-data purely?)
Into the clarity of notice (yes, a
Chair—here by the window; it is the back wall
Which is papered green; that is a piece of bare
Arm; and so forth). No—looking at the brightness,
Not as if down a tunnel of long darkness
—Itself, for all one knows, bored deep through light—but
As if separated from what one sees by
Only a pleasant spaciousness, glass or no
Glass. The distance no more contingent, perhaps,
Than that across which the dark mind looks out at
Bright windows of eye across the head from it,
I do not mind this slow watching in summer
Evenings. Nothing happening is by no means
Uneventful; and always the work goes on.

6/17 (TO GRUSHA)

No activity yesterday to suggest
Expanded coverage. He visited her
Saturday night, late, after his pickup, and
I covered her flat myself with the night shift.
This is meditative work. We were taught that
"Observation is an old man's memory"
And I think of this during the long hours of
Immobility, probing with dark unfelt
Fingers of infra-red light the corners of
Her room, the bathroom "seen" through the half-opened,
Mirrored door, the bed with two rumpled figures

Lumped into it—no, he has met no one else
Here: we are sure of that. "An old man's memory"
—Just so, memory is a ruined agent's
Succedaneum and prop: the work needs more
Than mere memory, more than the hard-edged, bright
Pictures we can focus on the details of.
But in this restful night work, when the pressure
Of the observer on the observed subject
Drops below the level of the soft brush of
Random winds, the pleasures of hope become those
Of memory. Each sharply delineated
New scene freezing into clarity in the
Night-glasses makes one feel "yes, this is how it
Was" rather than "Here it really is." The Foot
Does not appear to be using this address
For any obvious betrayals. We will
Continue to have him watched as before.

6/18 (TO GRUSHA)

Surveillance continues, and surveillance of
The surveillance in the usual way as
Well. There seems to be no need for my presence
On the site at this stage, and I have left it
All to the others. Tasks of observation
Can be demanding, and mistakes at every
Level are so easy to make—misreading,
At the level of the eyepiece cupping
The twinned transparencies of cornea
And glassy lens; misprision of those readings
By someone later on—not staring out of
Darkness toward light, but looking down in light
At the puzzle of half-truths on the desk-top.
A courier I knew once, Baker, liked to
Tell an exemplary tale of how for three
Months or so he had been using as a drop
A small, dim furnished room, checking in every
Day at various times, and staying there for
An hour or so. Each time, a piano would

Be playing in the room above his—sometimes
Tactfully exploring Chopin mazurkas,
Or wandering precisely through Scarlatti,
Sometimes climbing with less authority the
Major Beethoven peaks, sometimes relaxing
By a shallow but gleaming pool of cocktail
Standards—but in each case so perfectly
Submerged in its own style that Baker's attempt,
As he waited about, to frame a vision
Of the player, each day became more and more
Disturbing. Starting with the dancing hands, he
Would try to derive the rest from the music,
Arms, shoulders, sex, face, history, character.
For some weeks he struggled with this Protean
Inferential musician—it was throwing
His work off, and sometimes when miles away he
Would stop and listen to remembered playing
As if reminded of someone forgotten
For decades. Things went "from bad to worse". One day,
Maddened by the shapelessness of his fiction,
Determined to rub it out with fact, he ran
Upstairs, risking cover, work, everything, and
(Who was He-She? How did the various phases
Of so wide a life run into each other?)
Once on the upper landing, flung himself at
The appropriate door (from behind which there
Had been heard only silence for the past half-
Hour) pounded upon it, then, in unanswered
Rage, pushed past the minimal locking, entered
And found a room bare save for the piano,
Stool, table, lamp, and on the wall schedules of
Names and times for those who paid to practice there.
Baker was a mere courier and he stayed one.
This, too, was a message, his one adventure.

6/20 (TO GRUSHA)

Full reports on the observation of The
Foot should have reached you by the courier now.

How long is it since you supervised work like
This? Do you remember one's strange relation
To glass—the panes that blind, that distort objects,
The cool lenses that reveal them as they are?
I recall once watching across a street from
A safe house somewhere, through a closed window; the
Subject, a mild, wretched underwear jobber
Was teleported from his living room to
A neighbor's kitchen while I scratched my left ear:
An eye in a pane of glass is like a hole
In the mind—it tricks. "Love comes in at the mouth,"
But error, often, at the attentive eye.
Please forward all reports direct to Lyrebird.

6/21

The surveillance you ordered on The Foot has
Kept up; I have been reporting to Grusha
And there is yet no break in the case. Tonight
I visited the team at work across the
Street from his house in an empty apartment.
The silence, the darkness, the greenish fallen
Starlight of dials, the faintest humming, and all
About the pressure of tense men relaxing
At the long night's work. I thought of younger days
When I too spent nights with eyes and ears narrowed
To one source only. I remembered being
One of seven sleepers in a month-long cave
Of intense observation, emerging at
The project's end, palsied and trembling, into
Life—being good for no work for days and days.
It was not the simple fear of lost time that
Bothered us but rather observation's jail—
The traps that unencountered phenomena
Would set, to spring so slowly. We were warned in
Training, I remember, about absorption
In the observed image which might as well be
In a mirror. Do you also remember

One of the old set pieces for encoding
Back then in school—the one about the wise man
Who hid with his sons in a cave during an
Oppressive occupation of his country
—By the Romans, was it?—and lived and studied
Their sacred and nostalgic texts and footnotes
There devotedly. After several years they
Emerged in an unruptured world where men were
Farming as usual, doing their rounds of daily
Busy things. Disturbed, enraged, the teacher cried
Out: "These men turn away from eternity
To lower their heads toward the quotidian
Ground and her gross demands"—At which the entire
Prospect was directly consumed in burning,
The while from high above came an oversong,
A Voice from Heaven calling out "Did you come
To destroy my world? Back to your poor, blind cave!"
Do you remember that one? The mere touch of
Night work reminded me of it all again.

6/26 (TO GRUSHA)

This tedious surveillance goes on without
Any conclusive results, I should guess, for
Unless the simple reiteration of
Weeks and days and nights and months that adds up to
The simple checkerboard of The Foot's homely
Existence is itself some macro-cipher,
Then this observation should discontinue.
He takes his walks along the river and through
The wholesale districts, visits his little drops,
Leaves off, picks up, returns to his few pleasures
—The girl is, of course, totally clear, or blank,
Or whatever you wish—visits his mother
Each weekend an hour's railroad trip away:
I cannot see what may have gone wrong with him.
But then again, this is not for me to see:
I could be like the old courier Baker,

Save that perhaps by mere reason of knowing
His case to be exemplary . . . ? I too have
Misread—the One, in this case, for the Many:
Many years ago in a former stronghold
Of the double Empire, I was installed in
A cover office whose long windows gave on
One of those rich, small central European
City parks, wherein men only wandered in
The mornings, sometimes in groups, sometimes singly
And strangely meditatively; later on
Women in the evening hours would drift down
The same dark yellow gravel walks, and vanish
Among the same arches of hedge—again, some
With a serious solitude, some queerly
Animated in laughing or chattering
Groups. Was it the structure of the gardens which
So shaped the play of life in them? Did men find
The path through them on the way to work, women
The hush of windy vespers in the bushes?
One day I came across some correspondence
Of Monolith's—he had run the office some
Years before—remarking on how well-endowed
The small private asylum for the mildly
Insane next door must be. Since all the finest
Gardens are walled, you can see that my error
Was of no great consequence. Nevertheless,
I shall not risk an evaluation of
The Foot in the field. But let us get on with
Tying up the matter once and for all now.

6/27

Grusha has been receiving my reports in
The matter of The Foot; I cannot see why
This long and pointless surveillance must be drawn
Out still further. There is much work to be done.
I share, we all share, your sincere concern for
Security, and all this is part of the

Work itself, I know—but not a center, not
The intervening area, but perhaps
The periphery: it bounds and guards, but in
No way can constitute the matter of all
That we do. Well, then: the weather has closed in
And the little offshore affair that you wished
Me to look into for you shall have to wait
For a few days. Has Kidd reported in? I
Hope that he has—or, rather, that he has not:
Better that than that the situation be
So bad that you should have to keep it from me.

6/30

Nothing beyond routine. At the Museum
I may be asked to spend some time abroad next
Month: shall I go? Unless Orange has started,
Some of Maisie's people could handle day-to-
Day matters. But let me know soon. As for the
Offshore thing, the weather has not broken: small
Craft warnings are still up, and prospects for the
Next few days remain unsettled. Why do I
Find our need to depend still on something as
Messy and problematic as the weather
Somehow more reassuring than annoying?
I know I find that gluey impulse in me
Disturbing—all I can do is look to it.

6/30 (TO GRUSHA)

I thought I saw The Foot in the Museum
Yesterday, and I trembled for an instant
To think of how I had misjudged the vapid
Results of these weeks of intense observing—
He should by rights have had no business in that
Corridor leading toward the Conservation
Department—But then he turned his head slightly

And The Foot vanished, leaving not his double,
But you might say his half-again. Yes, it was
Most interesting: a whole three-quarter-view
Of him was that of The Foot, and yet the whole
Resemblance shattered in an instant and I
Wondered where the fragments had gone to. Mind you,
The probabilities are not in question
Here—bridge is a state of consciousness in which
The hand consisting of only the hearts seems
So astonishing, though equiprobable
With every unbiddable, nothing one; and
The work, contrariwise, leads us to expect
Only to be surprised. Perhaps one comes to
This mode of readiness early. I recall
How as a schoolboy I found reassurance
In oddnesses: a teacher, for example,
Inexplicably named Seneca Turner
(I knew him but slightly as a humorless
Ass) was well-known for his pomposities, and
One of my schoolmates was named Seneca, too
—Seneca Lerner, in fact. You may guess that
Lerner turned up in one of Turner's classes,
Filled out his name card, and provoked a siege of
Rage, threats against a student making fun of
A teacher's name, and so forth, until Lerner,
Fully as mortified, poor dear, produced all
Needed documents. The tale was told with wild
Relish by the other boys. But I brooded
Over the ghostly doubling of the name of
Old Latin wisdom with the Iroquoian
Tribe (whose name in Mohegan: *A'sinnika,*
Refers to "people of an ancient and still-
Standing stone")—I, who had Seneca problems
Enough, felt that this encounter was proper.
Surely for Seneca Turner the Lord had
Prepared a great, rhyming Seneca Lerner.
Whether, of course, the Lord had, We had, They had,
Was much the same. But perhaps I remember

53

This tiny matter only because the work
So molds the surfaces of our attention
That we can perceive ourselves in our as-yet-
Untuned childhoods. Still I cannot remember
That, even once, I felt that Senecas were
Being multiplied beyond necessity.

7/1

Kidd was seen today in the usual place.

7/1 (TO IMAGE)

Cupcake to Image: this new frequency is
Better I think for our little transmissions
And certainly free for use at the hour I
Am accustomed to using. The cipher, of
Course, remains the same old eleven-matrix.
Today at sending time my wrist just under
My watch was itching and burning as if it
Were keeping some canonical time other
Than what my watch recorded, as if it were
Ringing some pre-set alarm. I reached home in
Time to find the new frequency clear and I
Started a rapid encipherment of this
Small message, noticing how easily now
My plain text goes into a cipher like this,
So familiar with long use that I wonder
From time to time if it can still be secure.
It has a natural plainness of its own
By now. And yet I cling to it, thinking how
At any moment we might have to scrap it.
Agents should not have pets, nor grow fond of their
Ciphers: one-time pads, anonymous bedmates,
Momentarily adopted ladybugs—
These are for us, I should think, in the long run.

7/3 (TO GRUSHA)

Some of our people observing The Foot have
Complained of the new night-watching equipment—
The lenses, they say, while giving far better
Resolution than the older ones, make for
Greater distortion of another kind, a
Sort of flattening that, particularly
On the zoom, makes reading of the scene and its
Parts now more difficult, jamming those fragments
Of pattern up against a picture plane. They
Will soon learn to manage this, and the model
They implicitly build to describe the new
Phenomena of distortion—the terms from
Art—will recede into a conceptual
Darkness with their new routines of perception.
Just at the moment, though, the world is one bit
Stranger than it was before, as ever with
A temporary model of it that has
Not yet been disassembled. Thus consider
(As I did when a schoolboy) the accounts, all
Unacceptable to me, of why the moon's
Disc appears so much smaller at the zenith,
Distant and silvery, than when broad and red
—Like the first shield of some gigantic phalanx
Rising in hordes from behind the horizon.
Visual angles, atmospheric matters,
The scale that our cluttered horizons apply
To sources of phenomenon beyond them—
These hung uncomfortably about what I
Saw, and never blended into it. Then one
Day it all became clear—I abandoned the
Traditional picture (not of the Heavens,
Pretty, Keplerian, full of dotted lines
And false proportions of distance and size)
Of the huge, dark upended cereal bowl
Known in my childhood, on the inner surface
Of which stars clung a few planets wandered

And the mutable moon dependably moved.
In place of this I conjectured another
Fictional space—a dark paraboloid in
Place of the perfect hemisphere of old: a
Paraboloid against the inner side of
Which "the moon" journeyed, while all the rest of night's
"Tiny lamps" moved up and down a hemisphere—

(The model seems to have been something like this)

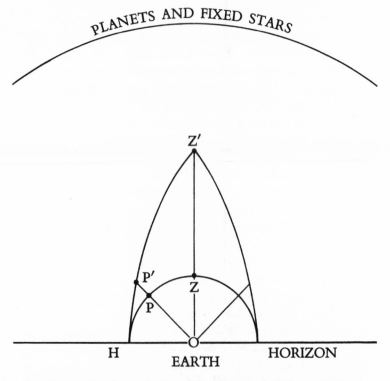

It will be seen that the moon's disc must travel the unequal distances H–P' and
P'–Z' in the same period (indeed in the same period as would be needed to
traverse the arcs H–P and P–Z in the old model). Hence the acceleration. The
speed at the Zenith stands to that at the Horizon as OZ'/ OH; the sizes in
the two positions are as OH / OZ'.

Much larger—of their own. The model showed how
The moon's disc, in the old fiction, would have to
Shrink from its size at H to that at Z, but
In my new model, moving from the same H
To Z′ more than twice the distance away,
The apparent disk would "shrink" naturally.
The constant circular velocity of
The old hemisphere-moon had of course to change
In an acceleration upward to the
Zenith, and then a slowing rate down again.
Thus equipped, I ventured out and forth the next
Clear night, and emboldened with my parable
Of a shield-size disc that ran away until
It looked no larger than a coin, I gazed up
Unto the dazzling clarity of darkness
And felt my vision propped up like a tower
Against the vast incomprehensible.
It was a parable as if of angels
Raining down spears of starlight, singing "Holy
Holy, Holy." This ridiculous picture
Gave me strength for some weeks until the clouds of
Certainty cleared; I knew the parabola
To be the path of nothing, then; that there was
Nothing in the world of which the model was
True. But for a few handfulls of days the night
Sky was domesticated without having
Been thereby shrivelled even at the edges.
I have always been grateful. Let the people
Doing surveillance each night struggle with their
Little fictional problems—The Foot, lighting
His cigarette, standing by the high bureau,
Looking too much like a poster showing The
Foot, lighting his cigarette etcetera;
The strangely shadowed infra-red images
Of rocking knees embracing a pale field of
Back, for a moment indecipherable
Because too much like arty cinema. They
Will learn to see the thing itself that looks too

Pictured as the thing itself again. Now
They remain in a harmless wild of wonder
For a while. They will go a bit more slowly,
But in the end—near ends and far—more surely.

7/4 (TO GRUSHA)

Lyrebird has thrown the switch on the surveillance
Of The Foot, and I am glad to be rid of
The responsibility—much might have gone
Wrong; but I shall never regret those nights of
Watching in darkness—or, after the project
Got under way, those nights of pondering
Alone in the darkness on the condition
Of the other agents I had assigned to
Watch in the darkness. Most of all, I shall miss
The opportunity to transmit on this
Seldom-used frequency, at such length. I may
Soon be leaving the region for a while, and
I doubt that it will be possible to be
In touch with you again. (We have no coded
Closings appropriate to what I want to
Say now, and all the profusion of phrases
Used in our various cover lives would sound
Like arch intrusions of a foreign language.)

7/8

All is in order for the trip. If Lyrebird
Needs to get through to me there the usual
Way—through Uncle Karl—will do. I await now
Your approval of the questionnaire I made
Up in case the opportunities present
Themselves. Most of all, I would really welcome
The chance, perhaps while there, to start up Orange
Again (Lamplight, after all, was supposed to

Be my main business this year). I now feel
That I can go ahead with it. And while the
Uncompleted matters seem tonight to crowd
Around me as I sit here enciphering:
The business of Kidd—can't I simply be
Told that I am not to be told about him?
The reasons for and outcome of the survey
Of The Foot—will it ever start up
Again? Lyrebird's suspended decision to
Take a much greater personal interest
In my case, or else to pass it over to
Someone else—while all these things hang in the air
Like some close, abiding beast of fog, still the
Prospect of the brief journey fills me with that
Sense of deep brightness behind surfaces that
We sometimes feel who have been quite cured of hope.

7/15 (TO IMAGE)

Same frequency, same cipher as you see, same
Mild, sad pleasure in these evening transmissions,
Swallows gathering the while on wires while
My floods of electromagnetic waves wash
Over and among them in a soundlessness
Lying below silence. For some time I have
Felt that this cipher would not be allowed me
For such extensive use for too much longer.
And yet, looking—not back with fondness, nor with
Desire ahead—but on, looking on at one's
Current work through crystallizing nostalgia:
This can be dangerous. *Do not look a gift
Cipher in the key* we were taught when young, and
I do not propose to go down hanging on
To this one when orders come to abandon
It. Some old cryptographer long ago, some
Visionnaire proposed once to hide messages
Enciphered in pictures of the midnight sky—

As if all the phenomenal stars were not
Already overloaded with hidden texts!
Floating specks in my eyes' deep space, the spots of
Darkness in the distance as other swallows
Gather outside other windows—all these soft,
Negative stars shift their encipherings from
Moment to moment: one must shun the madness
Of deeming them constant and significant.
So with this key which unlocks what eloquence
We have by locking up words in other words:
Let us transmit on it while yet we can, and
Move on in the end, move on then when we must.

7/15

I was followed yesterday—not on the way
To or from the Museum, but in it:
Crossing through two main galleries (a short cut
From Antiquities to my office) I found
Myself becoming aware of a cadence
Of footsteps echoing mine but out of phase
With the slight overhang of my rapid pace.
The galleries were nearly empty (it was
A few moments after opening). Have They
Put someone there? Let Lyrebrid know of this.
Whoever it was stopped following me when
I slipped behind a "No Admittance" door, but
I dare say there is something peculiar there.

7/16

A fine bright day. No one is following me
At the Museum. Cancel the message to
Lyrebird about it. None of Them is watching.

7/18

As from the airport where I have gone to check
On the placement of the pickup locker which
I shall use on my departure this weekend:
What crowds! as if the ordinary midweek
Needs of ordinary people to travel
Were like the pressure of a catastrophe—
Their faces are all full of the usual
Kinds of care, but from where I sit (not going
Anywhere today myself) their eyes all seem
To be the eyes of evacuees. I went
Home yesterday to find your new instructions
Awaiting me. Silence until departure.

7/20

All is quite ready for the trip tomorrow.
I shall make contact on the flight by means of
The playing-cards. But really! Solitaire! Is
Lyrebird on a holiday? Was this dreamed up
By some buffoon? I dislike, also, working
In such close quarters with an unknown—we must
Have cutouts but they must not manacle us—
And this Null to the Nullth power, this man with
The green handkerchief is too much an unknown.
He is not so much unknown territory,
An unmapped terrain, but rather like a null
Point on a good map—a notional town or
Village (like "Bishop's Piston" a few miles from
The real Piston Parva, or "West Japip")—to
Betray cartographic thieves who might pirate
The copyrighted map. A drop is one thing,
An impersonal agent is another.
Still, it will probably work out all right.

Via Green Handkerchief: The pickup at the
Airport went smoothly, and when I disembark
This message should be well on its way to you.
During the flight I played solitaire as if
Home at a table under a low-hanging
Chandelier surrounded by shadows, and, as
Always, playing with a silent partner there.
Playing patience is always playing patience
With death, opponent and partner both. But I
Was crowded into the humming, unshadowed
Cabin of a gray airplane, and the One with
The green handkerchief got the message from me,
Barely touching. Our eyes avoided our eyes.

Cupcake resuming transmission: it will be
Some days before the results of what was done
Over there will reach you; meanwhile the routines
Are gradually reabsorbing me now—
The drops visited, the haunts of my cover
Reentered, the whole of life familiarly
Closing around me as if all of life were
One thing only—as if in the midst of life
There were no work. Or rather—as I regard
The pleasant, late-summer crowd of shoppers I
Move among—as if the whole world perhaps were
At the work? What then? Why then there would be no
Need of it. No need at all. And the residues of
Its pockets, the traces of its energies
Would only be found in games and puzzles that
Children might play with and at, ever wisely
Uncurious about such things' origins.
But then I turn a corner into shadow
And a side-street, where the freest motions must

Needs at some time or other be furtive.
There is the work. There are very few of us.
I shall take over payments early next week.

8/22

This found in a long-since abandoned drop: a
Schematic sketch for some mysterious model,
Or model of a model. It shows a field
Or flat smooth surface bounded by a rim and,
Toward the lower left, an electromagnet.
At the upper right, a small, power-driven
Car is released on a free random travel;
The whole thing has been labelled "Homing Device"
With a notation saying that the car's speed
Shall decrease as an inverse function of the
Square of the distance of the car from the pole.
Is this some madman's simulation of a
State of stoic prudence? Or a sad picture
In need—in its poverty of picturing—
Of textual help (as a poor paragraph
Must have mute recourse to manual gestures
Like "Figure 1a.")? In any case I have
Sent the ridiculous thing by microdot.
It is most likely wholly irrelevant.

8/23

All seemingly well. I have seen Kidd and I
Wonder now at my wonderment at him then.
Riddle has been west and returned. Everyone
At the museum is pleased with what I came
Up with. There are no apparent problems. Why
Then should I have towards dawn this morning woken
To the most strange sounds of my own half-making:
What should have been merely the small clock clearly

Ticking at my bedside my hearing somehow
Decomposed into a two-part counterpoint
Of click and tocking and both their half-echoes
That seemed to come from different sources, one near,
One further away in the room behind me.
Then I awoke fully to a blending of
The two voices into the breathless hearsay
Of an alarm clock. Why should have I done this?
There was no need to rearrange so benign
An ordinariness, to avert as it
Were an ear. I woke up in no apparent
Alarm. The clock is quite unremarkable
As always. But perhaps this should be checked out.

8/25

Orange: it must not be abandoned; neither
Can I work on it, though. Thus Project Lamplight
Must abandon me. For want of Orange it
Should not fail. But I would not want to deceive
Myself that I could count on those flashes
Of understanding that would allow all the
Scraps and pieces and anxieties of the
Planning to catch fire all at one. Perhaps some
Controller, some extraordinary agent—
Soaring in the high region of his fancies,
With his garland and singing robes about him—
Might do it. Crowned only with a muss of hair,
Barely wrapped in the muffled tatters of my
Mute bathrobe I stare out at the gray early
Morning traffic groaning down its avenue.

8/26

Apologies for the last transmission: if
Orange cannot be set in motion, either

Some other time or agent will see it brought
About, or not, and that is all there is
To say about it. I should have included
Regular reports from the various drops, but
Nothing was new. Today at the Museum
A strange note crept into a discussion of
A loan exhibition: a new curator
Looked at me knowingly when suggesting that
He and I meet independently on the
Matter of some modern lithographs. Later,
Again, in his office, the telephone rang
And some dealer from Brussels engaged him for
Five tedious minutes; then, just before the
End of the conversation, he remarked—with
That same sidelong glance whipped out at me—"*Il
S'agit de l'oiseau lyre*". This may have been some
Redon print they were discussing. And it may
Have been a kind of overture from one of
Them, creeping out from under its cover. What
Instructions will there be in this matter? Our
Covers mutually enfold us, this man
And I, every day. I shall have to do something.

8/27

So. They may be at me soon to go over
To Them. If They were to approach me now, a
Prima facie proposition—or even
The subcutaneous virtue of a chance
To double against Them—it would only be
Useful and liberating for me to find
Out what I could. But, I suppose, for Lyrebird
Any such approach would be prima facie
Unattractive. Work in the field differs
So from work directing. We must be ready
To use the exciting flux of surfaces,
To lie in the momentary shade even
Of a dark trough of sea-wave, for instance, or

To walk the soft margins of a grassy track.
Lyrebird distrusts always the superstructure.
For him, Their move is Their move and if he could
Count on me as I do on myself there would
Never be need of anyone like Lyrebird.

8/28

False alarm. No move was made nor was there one
Intended as far as I can tell. All the
Knowing looks which I overread were merely
Sexual, the lyrebird was not Lyrebird, the
Whole notion issued forth fully armed from the
Hysteria of caution. The most diseased
Breeding place of all, as doubtless Lyrebird knows.

8/29 (TO IMAGE)

While I was away I missed your transmissions,
And mine to you, and now it appears that you
Must go off for a while beyond the range of
Equipment that it would be safe to use. Safe
Not just from Them, I mean; since I have never
Let Lyrebird know of my transmissions to you,
An intercepted message now would burn a
Receiver with the heat of its history.
Safer then, silence. Good luck on your journey.

9/1

Nothing new. Reports are desultory and
Inconclusive. Many minor agents seem
Fussily and quite unnecessarily
Preoccupied with procedural details.
I was twice asked for countersigns yesterday

In places where security has always
Lain in the surety of the casual,
In situations where a countersign called
For would seem just as preposterous as a
Counter-wonder or an identifying
Miracle asked for by one's secretary.
But the weather is strange and we have all been
On edge for more than a week now. All of us.

9/8

The last report sent by the microdots has
Reached you by now and I await instructions
For the new system. I have been at home with
A low-grade fever for a few days now and
Nothing can get to me through the Museum.
I have transmitted Lyrebird's instructions to
The other agents about holding off on
All reports for the next few days, but without
The slightest comprehension of the reason,
With so such to be done, for such an order.

9/11

In lieu of further orders I continue
To use this frequency, but merely to say
That I am still at home, that no new reports
Have reached me from further afield, and that the
Museum has gotten a temporary
Replacement for the next few weeks and I am
Under no pressure to return for a while.
Is there any special assignment for me?

9/12 (TO IMAGE)

I just heard that you had returned earlier
Than expected, and I hasten to greet you.
Your report, though yet incomplete, on Project
Alphabet is marvellous. From what I hear
Lyrebird will try to take some of the credit,
I know. But doing the work is what matters.
I have missed your messages, and even the
Sound, as it were, of your cipher recorded
Softly in my memory. Else a few days
Ago, I should have heard you at my ear, when
Newspapers told of the death of that poor wretch
So widely thought—and who believed herself—to
Be an agent. A closed garage, erratic
Behavior for some previous months—it may
Very well have been suicide. She was not
Even one of Theirs. "A lass, a lack" you might
Have muttered in my ear (implying that this
Sort of pseudo-work is ultimately
To be blamed on the posturings of Lac and
His ilk?) But here you are again. Let us get
Back to our own concerns, putting aside
Rumors of life, mere events (still, that woman . . .
I wonder what the chilly Lake said of it?)

9/13

Cupcake reporting. What can Lyrebird mean by
"A gift is on its way"? I ask for nothing
More than to do the work, to be able
To work. It is not given us to complete
It; neither are we free to desist from it.
I wish to be assigned a new frequency.

9/15 (TO LYREBIRD, DIRECTLY)

Your gift, the jigsaw puzzle full of yellow
And green arrived today and I have spread it
Out on the bare, varnished table top that is
Usually cluttered with books and papers.
Last year, a package reached me in a dream: I
Held it in my hand and heard myself thinking
"This is from Lyrebird". Something soft was inside
The wrappings. It was no gift. Then I awoke.
Your thoughtfullness now, at a bad time of year,
Will of course always be warmly remembered.
But any agent in the field must always
Take any sign as a rebuke even when
None may have been intended; to be able
To do this must be part of what strength we have.

9/17 (TO LYREBIRD)

Apologies for using this frequency.
The secret inks blot and run; the cipher is
Exasperating and its message boring.
The puzzle is not worth completing, and lies
In pieces, mostly. And even those pieces—
Pastel flashes floating on mahogany—
Glisten with blight, whatever the promise of
Their scatter might suggest washed away by the
Grossness of finishing: already a great
Bland frog sits croaking upon a violet
Lilypad in a large fragment of stagnant
Pool. Nor is he prince, nor is he watery
Shadow of some stone toad, nor cloud, nor beating
Heart of the biding hour, the gnat-clouded hour.
He fits as frog into no other puzzle,
His bulging plain text a reproach to all my
Daily twilight messages. Finish. Cupcake.

9/27 (TO IMAGE)

Dear Image: I picked up a strange transmission
Last night, but a dial being broken, could not
Determine whose frequency was being used.
It must be some superenciphered code of
Theirs (surely this did not come from you?). It read:
ET GLPKX ET VDI VXNT. I am puzzled.
Has someone of theirs—Lac perhaps—gone around
The bend again? Or is this the bungled work
Of one of ours? I know that one should never
Brood over transmissions not meant for oneself
Or one would go mad with reading noise alone,
Calculating symmetries of position
For pebbles on a windy beach. But there it
Is. But for what? What is to be done with it?

9/28 (TO IMAGE)

Image, your reply to my last transmission
Sounded unlike you—mechanical, rapped-out
On the wall of an adjoining cell, perhaps,
But not by a fellow-prisoner in it—
Only by a clockwork thing tapping away
In the checkerboard that prisoners use.
As for your suggestion that the strange message
Was a mistake—why am I unsatisfied?
Quickly—respond in the old way, for loss of
Image would be too much, now, to envision.

9/29

Addendum to the regular transmission:
One of their messages—ET GLPKX ET VDI
VXNT—resists further deciphering (it
Looks like some inscription about statues, but
No matter). Any help our cryptanalysts

Can give me with this will be rather welcome.
Meanwhile the routine reports keep drifting in,
And I pass them on with the appropriate
Evaluations, never breaking with the
Work's demands (else I should tell you each week that
Kidd is ridiculous, Riddle manic, Cram's
Eyes glued to his mirror, Prettyboy windblown).
But all I send you is in order. ET GLPKX
ET VDI VXNT: What is this all about?

9/30

This transmission sent out on all frequencies,
Encoded uncommonly; the superflux
Here is no dross, though, and I have sat watching
Key numbers in their serial dance growing
Further apart, outdistancing their touching,
Outstretched arms. Here, then, this, on all frequencies:

Open the codebook, decipher the message, and see
Essays in evasion disclose themselves: to tempt you,
Tea, muffins, jam, warm fire—and all that is unhappy
Sinks into the deep shadows in far corners, while here
Over the fireplace, dancing in the necromancy
Worked on the dead wood, paler shades of flame guard
    the edge
Of your brown study. Squibs snap from the logs. Outside,
    the
Paeans of meaningless wind rush past trees, shutters, *et
Ainsi de suite*. But how do you know that encoded
In those cycles of whining, the rise and fall of sigh,
There is not some message of mine—not of the work we
Are agents of, nor cover lives, but of breath itself.
Emphasis of breath: a hushed study in the decay
Of our material timber into its embers.
Echo of wind? Burletta of its urgency? Breath
Enwraps no messages, but of its aeromancy
There are no end of forms which, enciphered in twilight,

71

Are decoded in the blue morning air. The outside
Wind is an agency of breath. The low fire inside
Is an agency of rhyming death. Where is my breath?
Eeeee wheezes the respiring wind despairingly, *Eeee!*

10/1

(Lyrebird on all frequencies:

XXXXXXXXXXXXXXXX)

Notes

1/14 There was, indeed, little to "report" save that Cupcake had been revived from the prison of a small, ad hoc fiction. "Thumbtack," "Maisie," "The Foot" were hastily improvised code names. "Aspirin" was a different matter, "Allen Aspirin" being a name that Allen Ginsberg had glumly applied to himself one hung-over morning ca. 1949. I had no intention of encoding contemporary poets as spies in this first transmission.

1/15 "Steampump": W. H. Auden (see Introduction, p. ix).

1/17 "Kidd": Richard Howard, among poets one of my oldest friends. His *Untitled Subjects* (1969) and then *Two-Part Inventions* (1974) had confirmed his astonishing abilities in the art of dramatic monologue.

1/18 "Artifact": purely notional, as implied by his name.

1/19 (TO IMAGE)"Image": James Merrill (see Introduction, p. xii). I knew that the recipient of the messages to "Lyrebird" was neither receptive to nor interested in matters of poetic craft, of how the language of poetry forms, and is formed by, patterns. Also, I was beginning to see that for Cupcake—by nature digressive and prone to distraction—an excessive preoccupation with ciphers and other utensils of tradecraft could be his undoing in one way, even as his unauthorized communication with anyone other than Lyrebird would call for his eventual termination. By keeping faith with one obligation, Cupcake necessarily betrays another, as we all so often must. "Eleven by eleven grid": a device of encipherment, but here literally the eleven-syllable line in which the poem is composed; in the case of this message, eleven lines long.

1/19 "Felucca": notional.

1/20 (TO IMAGE) "Catullus." No agent known to the editor or to sources used as a cover name that of the first century Roman poet. The allusion may not be to the work, or it may be a superencipherment, a code-within-a-code.

1/21 "Gland": Adrienne Rich.

1/23 This meeting in a celebrated museum accords with Cupcake's cover life: he is an art historian and museum curator, as will be seen. Reproductions of the actual blue ceramic hippo were sold in the shop of the museum; the creature is known as "William."

1/24 "Moroz": Robert Frost.

1/26 "Sound of the lowest frequencies." This effect was indeed discovered accidentally, but in a high-frequency research laboratory: deaths caused by the low rumbles of some faulty air-conditioning equipment were misattributed, perhaps because of all the researchers' attention to supersonics and their tactical possibilities. No recent work on this has turned up. "Thumbtack": notional.

1/27 "Turn spool . . ." These "refrains" were enciphered simply as "turn" after the first one. Theocritus II *"Magical whirligig, fetch to my house my unfaithful beloved."*

1/28 In this case, the form of the transmission is a pastoral dialogue.

1/30 "Riddle": Daryl Hine.

2/4 "Kidd": see note to transmission 1/17.

2/5 "Heavy with sweet news." Is there possibly some super-encipherment here? There may be some connection with a biblical passage used as another kind of code (*Numbers* 13).

2/6 And subsequently "Project Lamplight" [see also, subsequently, Projects Orange, Red, and Blue]: this concerned "Spectral Emanations," my long poem in seven parts, each titled after the name of one of the colors of the solar spectrum, in progress 1973-76.

2/9 "Tallman": Stephen Spender.

2/18 "Kakeidoscope" (sic!).

2/20 "Rembrandt etching." This one is commonly called "Faust in His Study."

2/21 "Pike": Anthony Hecht; "Prettyboy": W. S. Merwin.

3/2 "Project Lilith": my poem *The Head of the Bed,* published as a chapbook in 1974.

3/8 (TO IMAGE) [Scrawled on the worksheets of the decipherer here, the phrase "mute poesies" (?)].

4/3 (TO IMAGE) Cupcake's obsessions with encipherment, and, later on, with night surveillance, seem to emanate from a common source in the agent's perplexing psyche.

4/6 "Cram": Mark Strand; "Lac": Robert Lowell.

4/10 "Aunt Clara": notional—in any event, a piece of tradecraft, rather than a person.

4/16 *"The length of things . . . joy"*: George Santayana, "Skylarks." "Flypaper": notional.

4/17 "Lake": Elizabeth Bishop.

4/30 The punctuation (bracketing, etc.) is conjectural and, of course, as throughout, editorial.

5/1 (TO IMAGE) Again, possible superencipherment? Some trace of the Indo-European root seems to occur in each "line."

5/9 "Project Aspasia": the libretto for Hugo Weisgall's opera, *Jenny, or The Hundred Nights*. "Kilo"; "Puritan"; etc.: see Introduction, pp. vii, xv.

5/11 "Project White": notional. It might be thought of as a vast, general blanking-out operation—among other things, a negation of the poetry and the imagination generally.

5/12 "Claus of Innsbruck": a notional sculptor in Browning's "My Last Duchess."

5/12 (TO IMAGE) "Null." A "null" is a cipher letter or figure inserted into a text merely to confuse. It has no plain meaning; it stands for nothing. That the agents here designated as nulls should be notional seems highly unlikely—Cupcake's controlling people would never stand for so much ambiguity and waste. It will be noted that Image (see note to transmission 1/19) is not listed as a null, nor, indeed, is "Bun."

5/13 "Ember": John Ashbery.

6/1 (TO IMAGE) "M": Martha Hollander; "Decay": David Kalstone.

6/15 (TO BUN) "Bun." (?) This isolated transmission seems quite inexplicable. It is not even known whether "Bun" is actually an agent.

6/16 And subsequently (TO GRUSHA) "Grusha": Richard Poirier.·

6/18 (TO GRUSHA) "Baker": a friend, not a writer, now deceased.

6/26 (TO GRUSHA) "Monolith": Albert Einstein.

6/30 (TO GRUSHA) The "Turner" and "Lerner" are fictional substitutes for the rhyming surnames of two actual Senecas, a student and a teacher at my high school.

7/3 (TO GRUSHA) The points designated "H" and "Z" obviously stand for Horizon and Zenith respectively; it is not hard to deduce the position of "Z′." A graphic representation of the model has been inserted *in situ*.

7/8 "Uncle Karl": Karl Miller.

9/12 "Project Alphabet": Merrill's "The Book of Ephraim," later comprising the first section of his *The Changing Light at Sandover*. The "poor wretch" was Anne Sexton.

9/13 "Complete . . . desist." *Pirke Aboth* 2:20?

9/17 This transmission was originally written as a separate poem, entitled "Cupcake to Lyrebird" (see Introduction, pp. vii–viii).

9/27 "ET GLPKX . . . etc." This is evidently a cipher-key. It seems astonishing that Cupcake might not have guessed this, although it looks at first glance to be itself an enciphered message. Elementary keys are usually memorable bits of plain text, like names or first lines of poems (e.g. "The eye's plain version is a thing apart"), or proverbs (e.g. "Expect poison from the standing water").

9/28 All that can be gathered about Image's transmissions comes from Cupcake's own material. As this record was being prepared, a number of cryptic and very brief messages in the characteristic cipher came to light. They had obviously been intercepted by other sources. Identified only by dates, they might indeed have come from Image. But perhaps not. Four examples are:

2/1 Artifact underground? Good griddance. Prepare
Detectors (yours and mine) for field-day. Image.

2/12 Here's "Judy's" book. I cypher you and ball some.

6/16 Commoner sense, dear Cupcake, is the hardened
Pretender. Non-signs betrays lies' majesty.

n.d. Cupcake—mere crumbs upon a smiling lip? No,
Fixed in disk the wishful taper o'er him shines.

These "transmissions" from Image were all actually sent me by James Merrill (the mode of punning here being obviously his). The agent whom he named "Judy" was the writer Judith Moffett, one of whose books accompanied this monostich.

9/30 "This transmission sent out . . . etc." This disturbing and disturbed transmission seems to be a kind of cry for help. But to whom? The "superflux" in the ensuing message can be identified as the two extra syllables per line—all the Cupcake transmissions decode as purely hendeca-syllabic. Taking the first and last as significant additions, we look for a cipher using them and find nothing. But following the hint about the "serial dance," etc., we can take the lines numbered

1, 2, 3, 5, 8, 13, 21

—or the sequence of integers in the almost proverbial Fibonacci series (in which each term is the sum of the two preceding ones). Then, reading down the left, we get on those lines the initial syllables

O Es Tea O Pae Em Eeeee

—or, as the names of letters in the English alphabet,

O S   T O P M   E

(like the vulgar cry of a crazed killer reported gleefully in the tabloids: "Stop me before I kill yet again"). Similarly, on the terminal syllables,

See you py cy et cay Eeee, or C U P C A K E

Ingenious. But to whom? To whom?

The last message from Lyrebird, "XXXXXXXXXXXXXXXXX," when keyed by the mysterious text sent earlier, is easily deciphered on a Vigenère tableau like the one below. The key letters give in turn the cipher alphabet in which each letter of the message is coded—each "X," that is. Thus, the first "X" is in the cipher alphabet beginning with "E" (look down the left-hand margin for the alphabet in question); locate the "E" alphabet (fifth from the top), find "X" in it, and read up vertically in the same column until you find the lower-case letter heading the column (here, "t"). And so on.

10/1 If deciphered by the method detailed above, this message from Lyrebird, presumably to anyone listening, reads *"TERMINATE CUPCAKE,"* and constitutes a sort of open contract. It was duly executed.

	a	b	c	d	e	f	g	h	i	j	k	l	m	n	o	p	q	r	s	t	u	v	w	x	y	z
A	A	B	C	D	E	F	G	H	I	J	K	L	M	N	O	P	Q	R	S	T	U	V	W	X	Y	Z
B	B	C	D	E	F	G	H	I	J	K	L	M	N	O	P	Q	R	S	T	U	V	W	X	Y	Z	A
C	C	D	E	F	G	H	I	J	K	L	M	N	O	P	Q	R	S	T	U	V	W	X	Y	Z	A	B
D	D	E	F	G	H	I	J	K	L	M	N	O	P	Q	R	S	T	U	V	W	X	Y	Z	A	B	C
E	E	F	G	H	I	J	K	L	M	N	O	P	Q	R	S	T	U	V	W	X	Y	Z	A	B	C	D
F	F	G	H	I	J	K	L	M	N	O	P	Q	R	S	T	U	V	W	X	Y	Z	A	B	C	D	E
G	G	H	I	J	K	L	M	N	O	P	Q	R	S	T	U	V	W	X	Y	Z	A	B	C	D	E	F
H	H	I	J	K	L	M	N	O	P	Q	R	S	T	U	V	W	X	Y	Z	A	B	C	D	E	F	G
I	I	J	K	L	M	N	O	P	Q	R	S	T	U	V	W	X	Y	Z	A	B	C	D	E	F	G	H
J	J	K	L	M	N	O	P	Q	R	S	T	U	V	W	X	Y	Z	A	B	C	D	E	F	G	H	I
K	K	L	M	N	O	P	Q	R	S	T	U	V	W	X	Y	Z	A	B	C	D	E	F	G	H	I	J
L	L	M	N	O	P	Q	R	S	T	U	V	W	X	Y	Z	A	B	C	D	E	F	G	H	I	J	K
M	M	N	O	P	Q	R	S	T	U	V	W	X	Y	Z	A	B	C	D	E	F	G	H	I	J	K	L
N	N	O	P	Q	R	S	T	U	V	W	X	Y	Z	A	B	C	D	E	F	G	H	I	J	K	L	M
O	O	P	Q	R	S	T	U	V	W	X	Y	Z	A	B	C	D	E	F	G	H	I	J	K	L	M	N
P	P	Q	R	S	T	U	V	W	X	Y	Z	A	B	C	D	E	F	G	H	I	J	K	L	M	N	O
Q	Q	R	S	T	U	V	W	X	Y	Z	A	B	C	D	E	F	G	H	I	J	K	L	M	N	O	P
R	R	S	T	U	V	W	X	Y	Z	A	B	C	D	E	F	G	H	I	J	K	L	M	N	O	P	Q
S	S	T	U	V	W	X	Y	Z	A	B	C	D	E	F	G	H	I	J	K	L	M	N	O	P	Q	R
T	T	U	V	W	X	Y	Z	A	B	C	D	E	F	G	H	I	J	K	L	M	N	O	P	Q	R	S
U	U	V	W	X	Y	Z	A	B	C	D	E	F	G	H	I	J	K	L	M	N	O	P	Q	R	S	T
V	V	W	X	Y	Z	A	B	C	D	E	F	G	H	I	J	K	L	M	N	O	P	Q	R	S	T	U
W	W	X	Y	Z	A	B	C	D	E	F	G	H	I	J	K	L	M	N	O	P	Q	R	S	T	U	V
X	X	Y	Z	A	B	C	D	E	F	G	H	I	J	K	L	M	N	O	P	Q	R	S	T	U	V	W
Y	Y	Z	A	B	C	D	E	F	G	H	I	J	K	L	M	N	O	P	Q	R	S	T	U	V	W	X
Z	Z	A	B	C	D	E	F	G	H	I	J	K	L	M	N	O	P	Q	R	S	T	U	V	W	X	Y